e ISLAND of NANTUCKET

016.91744
C65h   71561

DATE DUB			

GAYLORD M-2   PRINTED IN U.S.A.

The History
of
NANTUCKET ISLAND
A Bibliography
of
Source Material
with
Index and Inventory

Compiler
Marie M. Coffin
Nantucket Island, Massachusetts

Another Publication
of
Nantucket Historical Trust
Nantucket, Massachusetts

DEDICATION

Dedicated to everyone everywhere
who would like to learn more about
the history of our great country.

Introduction

The Nantucket Historical Trust holds among its foremost objectives the enrichment of knowledge about this marvelous island. Preserving these things that have made Nantucket a unique, warm, friendly, and thoroughly American landmark requires the ambitious energy and sincere devotion of many people.

This book, therefore, is really the work of a living force, directing its scholarly pursuit toward making Nantucket come to life wherever these pages find a home. The Trustees owe thanks to many helpful and interested friends of the Island, but above all their thanks and all credit go to Mrs. Charles Clark Coffin of Nantucket for her unrelenting and excellent work in compiling the elements of this Bibliography.

Our Island is, indeed, wonderful. It is best known as having been the world's largest whaling port. The student and the researcher will find untold treasure in Nantucket's history. No landmark deserves greater respect as a symbol of our American heritage, for its place in the origin of our nation, and for its contribution to the life and livelihood of that special breed of people known as New Englanders.

To you who share our personal appreciation for Nantucket, and an interest in American History, this work will serve to document a multitude of familiar and well-loved material. To those who search here for a first insight into Nantucket's historical glory "Welcome aboard!" Someday we hope you will come to visit this "Far Away Island" and capture in person a feeling for its special place in American History.

The Trustees of
Nantucket Historical Trust

Henry B. Coleman

George W. Jones

Mary Ann Beinecke

Walter Beinecke, Jr.

K. Dun Gifford

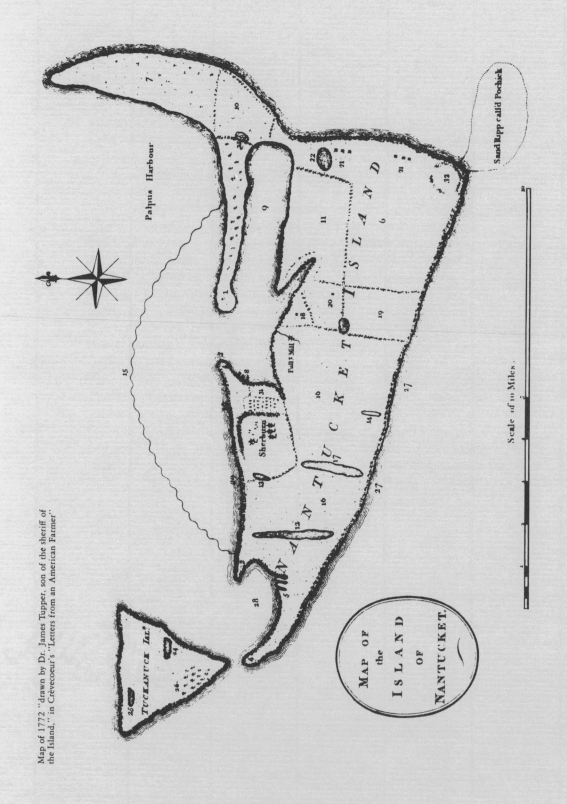

Map of 1772 "drawn by Dr. James Tupper, son of the sheriff of the Island," in Crèvecoeur's "Letters from an American Farmer"

MAP of the ISLAND of NANTUCKET.

Scale of 10 Miles.

Papus Harbour

Sand Rupp call'd Porbick

NANTUCKET ISLAND

Sherbourn

Fulls Mill

TUCKANUCK Isl?

Preface

The need for a definitive source of information that catalogues all the known data pertaining to the history of Nantucket Island has long been recognized by those with a real interest in this historical landmark, discovered in 1602.

As the logical organization to undertake such a task, the Nantucket Historical Trust began in 1968 accumulating detailed information on all the material that could be discovered. The present location has been described wherever possible. The result is, so far as can be determined, the first Bibliography of Source Material on the History of Nantucket Island.

Covered in this work is an inventory of important documents, old maps and charts, portraits and pictures, scrapbooks, logbooks and records of various kinds having to do with the island of Nantucket and its historical past. It is the purpose of the Nantucket Historical Trust to preserve in this manner a cataloguing of invaluable material, much of which might otherwise be lost, forgotten, or destroyed.

The task is unending. Excellent work is underway on Nantucket at the Atheneum Library and the Whaling Museum microfilming important Nantucket data in their possession. This includes the well-known collection of scrapbooks owned by Miss Grace Brown Gardner, whose help and cooperation in this project is greatly appreciated.

Marie M. Coffin

Marie M. Coffin
Compiler

Explanation and Abbreviations

EXPLANATION
    In Parenthesis—*Where Located*
    In Quotation Marks—*Has been published, usually in book form*

ABBREVIATIONS
    Athen.—*Atheneum Library, Nantucket, Mass.*
    N.H.A.—*Nantucket Historical Association*
    Proc.—*Proceedings of N.H.A.*
    Bull.—*Bulletins of N.H.A.*
    Fair St. Museum—*Fair Street Museum of N.H.A.*
    Whal. Museum—*Whaling Museum of N.H.A.*
    H.A.B.S.—*Historic American Buildings Survey, Department of the Interior, Washington, D.C.*
    Crosby Coll.—*Collection of Everett U. Crosby, owned by Mrs. Marie M. Coffin, Nantucket, Mass.*
    G.B.G. Scrapbooks (micro. Athen.)—*Grace Brown Gardner's Scrapbook Collection, all on microfilm at Atheneum*
    Hist. Nant.—*Historic Nantucket, a Quarterly Publication of Nantucket Historical Association*
    Hist. Trust—*Nantucket Historical Trust*
    I. & M.—*Inquirer and Mirror, Nantucket, Mass.*
    Lib. Cong.—*Library of Congress, Washington, D.C.*
    M. M. Library—*Library of the Maria Mitchell Association, Nantucket, Mass.*
    Micro.—*Has been microfilmed*
    Soc. Pres. N. E. Antiq.—*Society for the Preservation of New England Antiquities, Boston, Mass.*

A

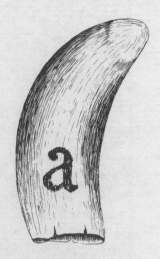

ACCOUNT BOOKS, EARLY
See Journals
See Logbooks

ACTORS ON NANTUCKET
'Sconset Actor Colony—*Recording by Fawcett, 1959 (N.H.A.)*
'Sconset Actor Colony—*Recording by Everett, 1959 (N.H.A.)*
Actors on the Island During 'Sconset's Heyday—*Hist. Nant. Oct. 1962*
"Sconset Heyday"—*Barnes, The Island Press, 1969*
Theatre Workshop, Nantucket—*Workshop Files & Publicity*

ADAMS, NANCY STORY
Nancy Adams—*Hist. Nant., Apr. 1968*

AGRICULTURE
Agriculture—*"The Island of Nantucket", Godfrey, 1882, p. 8*
Records of the Nantucket Agricultural Society for Years 1860-1918, and
    Treasurer's Accounts 1856-1895 (Store-room Fair St. Museum)
Soil Survey of Dukes and Nantucket Counties—*Latima, Bureau Chemistry and
    Soils, U.S. Dept. Agriculture, 1925*
Agricultural Society—*see Organizations*
See Farming
See Industries

AIRPORT AND AIR TRANSPORT
Airport—*Records of Airport Commission, Nantucket, Mass.*
Air Transport in its Early Days—*Hist. Nant., Apr. 1957*
Nantucket Airport—*"Argument Settlers", Turner, 1966, p. 137, 147, 163*
See Plane Crashes

ALMANACS
New England Town and Country Almanack, 1769 (micro. Athen.)
Almanack or Astronomical Diary—*Nathaniel Ames, 1751-1770 (micro. Athen.)*

ANECDOTES
See Sayings and Customs

ANIMALS
Animals, including Shearing—*Vol. 3, G.B.G. Scrapbooks (micro. Athen.)*
Prairie Dogs—*"Argument Settlers", Turner, 1966, p. 69*
Horses—*see Transportation*

ARGUMENT SETTLERS

9 published editions: 1917; 1920; 1924; 1926; 1936; 1944; 1946; 1959; 1966—*Turner, I. & M. Press*

ARTIFACTS

"Nantucket Indian Artifacts"—*Shurrocks, I. & M. Press, 1940*
Shurrocks Collection (Fair St. Museum)
Dunham Collection (Fair St. Museum)
See Archaeology
See Indians

ARTISTS

Nantucket Artists (with location of pictures) including the following: Phebe Fitzgerald Barney; Elizabeth Rebecca Coffin; Anne Ramsdell Congdon; George Fish; Annie Barker Folger; James Walter Folger; Sally Gardner; J. S. Hathaway; Eastman Johnson; Wendell Macy; George Marshall; Alexander Seaverns; Smibert; Anna Swain; William Swain; Benjamin Tobey—*Stark, Hist. Nant. July. 1958; Oct. 1958 and Apr. 1959.*
Painters Who Have Worked at Nantucket in the Past—*Coffin, 1968 (Athen.)*
Loan Exhibition of Edgar W. Jenney Water Colors—*Metropolitan Museum of Art, N.Y. Bull. Nov. 1940*
"An American Genre Painter, Eastman Johnson"—*Bauer, 1940*
"Eastman Johnson at Nantucket"—*Crosby, 1944*
Phebe Folger's Water Colors—*Hist. Nant., Oct. 1966*
Art and Artists—*"The Island of Nantucket", Godfrey, 1882, p. 15*

ASSESSORS

Maps of Sections of Nantucket and Siasconset made by Wm. F. Codd in 1908 and brought up to date (Assessors' Office, Town of Nantucket)
Card Index of Owners of all Property, Resident and Non-Resident (Assessors' Office, Town of Nantucket)

ASSOCIATIONS

See Organizations and Clubs

ASYLUM

See Poor Farm
See Quaise

ATHENEUM

Microfilmed Material at Atheneum—*see lists under Books, Census, Logbooks, and Scrapbooks, etc.*
"Catalogue of the Atheneum Library With its Rules and Regulations"—*Hussey & Robinson, Nantucket, 1883 (Athen.)*
Great Hall—*Hist. Nant., Apr., 1957*
Catalogue of Paintings, Prints, Maps and Other Objects at Atheneum, with descriptions and locations, as prepared in 1966 (Athen.)
Atheneum at Time of 1846 Fire—*N.H.A. Proc. 1949, p. 38*
See Maps
See Paintings
See Ship Models
See Prints

AUCTIONS

Auction Sales Book 1847 (micro. Athen.)

AUDUBON AT NANTUCKET

Audubon—*N.H.A. Proc. 1942, p. 26-30 and Hist. Nant., Apr. 1957, p. 14*

AUTOMOBILES

Nantucket's Automobile Controversy—*"100 Years on Nantucket", I. & M. 1921*

B

BAKER, REV. LOUISE S.

Memorial to Rev. Baker—*Foreword by Harry B. Turner in "Eunice Hussey",
written by Rev. Baker in 1895. I. & M. Press, 1938*
Reverend Louise S. Baker—*New York Daily Tribune, Dec. 21. 1884*

BAND

Nantucket Brass Band, Record of, 1856-1860 (Crosby Coll.)

BANKS

"Robbery of the Nantucket Bank"—*Wm. Coffin & Albert Gardner, 1816 (Athen.)*
Manufacturers & Mechanics Bank, Embezzlement of $130,000—*Broadside from
Mirror Office, June 4, n.d. (probably 1844)*
"Trial of Barker Burnell, Cashier of Manufacturers & Mechanics Bank,
Nantucket"—*Mussey & Co., Publishers, Boston, 1847 (Athen.)*
Citizens Bank Stock 1831-1842 (micro. Athen.)
Banks—*"The Island of Nantucket", Godfrey, 1882*
Pacific National Bank, History of—*N.H.A. Proc. 1904*
Nantucket Bank Robbery in "Wm. Mitchell of Nantucket", N.H.A. Proc. 1949
Nantucket Bank Robbery in 1795—*Nantucket Town Crier, Jan. 23, 1948*
150th Anniversary Pacific National Bank, I.&M. Press, 1954
Photograph of early painting, c. 1820, of Pacific Bank (Fair St. Museum)
New Savings Bank Opened on Orange Street—*"Argument Settlers", Turner,
1966, p. 106*

BAR

See Jetties

BARNEY

Barney, Matthew—*N.H.A. Proc. 1946*
Barney Papers—*see Genealogy*

BASKETS, LIGHTSHIP

See Industries

BELL

Old Bell—*"The Island of Nantucket", Godfrey, 1882, p. 237*
Nantucket's Famous Bell—*"100 Years on Nantucket", I.&M., 1921*
Old South Church Bell—*Recording by Jay Gibbs (N.H.A.)*
The Portuguese Bell—*Various leaflets of Second Congregational Meeting-
House Society, Nantucket (Unitarian Church)*
Portuguese Bell—*Nantucket Town Crier, Sept. 19, 1947*

BIBLES

Very old Gardner Family Bible, 1762 (Mrs. Lewis S. Edgarton, Nantucket,
Mass.)
Nantucket Family Bibles—*See list of these and where owned in "Vital Records
of Nantucket to Year 1850", published by New England Historical Genea-
logical Society, Boston, 1925 (Athen.)*
200 or more Nantucket Family Bibles (Whaling Museum)
Obed Macy's 4 volume Bible (Fair St. Museum)
Family Bibles (Listed in files at Fair St. Museum) (Kept in Store-room at Fair
St. Museum)

BICYCLE CLUB

Bicycle Supplement—*I. & M. June 13, 1896*

BIRDS

Ornithology—"*The Island of Nantucket*", *Godfrey, 1882, p. 240*
Migration of Birds—*Circular 16, Fish & Wildlife Service, U.S. Dept. of Interior*
"Summer Birds of Nantucket"—*Mason, Mass. Audubon Soc. Bull. n.d.*
"A Preliminary List of Birds of Nantucket"—*Brooks, 1929. M.M. Publication*
Journal of Audubon 1840-43, Cambridge Hist. Soc. 1929
Audubon at Nantucket—*N.H.A. Proc. 1941*
Some Late Summer Birds of Nantucket—*Meade, Mass. Audubon Soc. Bull., June, 1942*
"The Birds of Nantucket"—*Griscom & Folger, 1948*
"Birds Are Her Beat"—*Look Magazine, Sept. 13, 1960*
"Bird Tracks on Nantucket"—*Coffin, 1966*
"The Goldfinch Story"—*Coffin, 1967*
"The Outer Lands"—*Sterling, 1967*
Birds—*Vol. 3, G.B.G. Scrapbooks (micro. Athen.)*
See Hunting

BLACKFISH

Nantucket Visited by Four Schools of Blackfish—"*100 Years on Nantucket*", *I. & M. 1921*

BOATS AND BOATMEN

Nantucket's Boatmen of Other Days—*Crowley, "100 Years on Nantucket", I. & M. 1921*
See Steamers
See Whaleships

Nantucket Visited by Four Schools of Blackfish—"*100 Years on Nantucket,*"

BOOKS, NANTUCKET

"Books and Baskets, Signs & Silver of Old-Time Nantucket"—*Crosby, 1940*
"Nantucket in Print"—*Crosby, 1946*
Collections of books relating to Nantucket may be found in Atheneum; Library, Vault and Vestibule bookcase at Fair St. Museum; Whaling Museum; Soc. Pres. N.E. Antiquities, Boston; John Carter Brown Library, Providence, R.I.; Yale University Library; Library of Congress, Washington, D.C., etc. Also many collections privately owned in Nantucket.
Nantucket Books—*Vol. 5 G.B.G. Scrapbooks (micro. Athen.)*
Nantucket Books on Microfilm at Atheneum include the following:
"Letters From an American Farmer"—*Crévecoeur, 1782*
"List of Persons from Nantucket Now in California"—*Brock, 1850*
Addendum to "Starbuck" and "Whaling Masters"—*Hegarty, 1964*
"Survey of Nantucket Harbor, 1803-1804"

"Captain Prescott and the Opium Smugglers"—*Stackpole*
"The Yankee Whaler"—*Ashley*
"The Ocean"—*Gosse*
"Sailor Charley, or Life in a Whaler"
Mrs. Ricketson's Whaling Journal 1871-1874
"Ten Days in Nantucket"—*Gould*
"The Marine Mammals"—*Scammon*
"China Trade Post-Bag"—*Loines*
"Some Recollections"—*Low*
"Bits of China"—*Hunter*
For other material microfilmed at Atheneum to date, see:
Almanacs; Cookbooks; Journals; Logbooks; Maria Mitchell's Notes; Sanford
Material; Scrapbooks of Grace Brown Gardner.
See Bibles
See History of Nantucket

BOSTON TEA PARTY
Nantucket's Connection With—*N.H.A. Proc. 1922*

BOTANY
See Flora and Fauna

BUILDINGS
Buildings in Nantucket for which measured drawings, historical data and photo-
graphs have been prepared for the Historic American Buildings Survey, Dept.
of the Interior, Washington, D.C., through the cooperation of the Nantucket
Historical Trust, are:
Congregational Church
North Vestry
Masonic Lodge Bulding (back of Pacific Bank)
Coffin-Athearn Stores (old Town Bldg.)
Atheneum
3 Bear St., Bunker House
Maria Mitchell Birthplace, 1 Vestal St.
21 Union St.
33 Milk Street
75 Main St.
94 Main St.
1 North Water St. (taken down)
Unitarian Church
Macy Warehouse (Kenneth Taylor Galleries)
Whaling Museum
Odd Fellows Bldg. on Centre St.
African Meeting House, Pleasant & York Sts.
Josiah Coffin House, Cliff Rd.
14 Orange St.
Straight Wharf Theatre
Many more have been photographed and historical data finished, but measured
drawings not yet completed. These include:
Dell House, Academy Lane
Methodist Church
51 Centre St. (Folger House)
52 Centre St. (Joshua Coffin House)
30 Hussey St.
12 Liberty St.
Pacific Club Bldg.
Pacific Bank Bldg.
69 Main St.
72 Main St.
77 Main St.
89 Main St.

93, 95 and 97 Main St. (Three Bricks)
96 Main St.
99 Main St.
105 Main St.
107 Main St.
111 Main St.
117 Main St.
139 Main St.
153 Main St.
11 Mill St.
11 Milk St.
35 Milk St.
4 New Dollar Lane
4 North Water St.
5 Orange St.
Orange St. Block
33 Orange St.
53 Orange St.
8 Pine St.
19 Pleasant St.
32 W. Chester St. (Richard Gardner House)
Jared Coffin House
Fish Houses as a Group
Oldest House
Surfside Life Saving Station
Elihu Coleman House
Tashama Farm
"Shanunga", 'Sconset
"Auld Lang Syne", 'Sconset
(On file at Athen.; N.H.A.; Lib. Cong.)

Mass. Catalogue H.A.B.S.—*Published by Sec. of Commonwealth, Boston, Mass., 1964*

Blueprints for restoration of Jethro Coffin House, measured and drawn by Alfred F. Shurrocks, 1927; sketch plans for alterations of house on Gull Island, 1928; 8 Blueprints for alterations and addition to Moor's End, by Prof. Fiske Kimball, 1927—*(Fair St. Museum, being copies made by Nantucket Historical Trust from originals at Soc. Pres. N.E. Antiq., Boston)*

Ancient Buildings—*Worth, N.H.A. Bull., Vol. 1, Bull. 1; and Vol. 2, Bull. 7*

House Lots of Settlers—*N.H.A. Bull., Vol. 2, Bull. 2*

Original Lay-Outs on Harbor—*N.H.A. Bull., Vol. 2, Bull. 4.*

Early Houses at Nantucket—*N.H.A. Proc. 1904, p. 19-24*

The Early Dwellings of Nantucket—*Schweinfurth, White Pine Series, Vol. 111, No. 6, 1917*

Historic Buildings—*"Nantucket's Centennial Celebration"—Dudley, 1895*

Big Shop —*N.H.A. Proc. 1916*

The Starbuck Brick Houses on Main Street—*"100 Years on Nantucket", I. & M. 1921*

"Three Bricks and Three Brothers"—*Gardner, 1945*

Oldest House—*see Oldest House*

1800 House—*see Eighteen Hundred House*

Hadwen House-Satler Memorial—*see Hadwen House*

Development of the New England Dwelling-House—*Worth, in Lynn Hist. Soc. publication 1910*

Nantucket Notebook—*House & Garden, July 1948*

Jared Coffin House—*see Jared Coffin House*

Houses—*"Nantucket Guide", Godfrey, 1882., p. 231*

"Old Houses of New England"—*Mixer, 1927*

Some Early Dwellings in Nantucket—*"Nantucket: a History", Douglas-Lithgow, 1914*

"Rambling Through the Streets and Lanes of Nantucket"—*Stackpole, 1947 and 1951*

Main Street's Buildings—*William F. Macy, 1935 (pamphlet compiled for Hospital Fete)*
"Ninety Five Per Cent Perfect"—*Crosby, 1937*
"Old Houses on Nantucket"—*Duprey, 1959*
"A Mirror of Nantucket"—*Fowlkes, 1959*
Buildings—*Vol. 5 and 7 G.B.G. Scrapbooks (micro. Athen.)*
Nos. 65, 67 and 69 Main St. —*Hist. Nant. Apr. 1964*
Collection old Stereoptican Views of Nantucket Houses—*(Fair St. Museum and Library of Soc. Pres. N.E. Antiq.)*
6 loose-leaf albums of pictures of Nantucket houses, c. 1895, made from Turner Collection of plates (Fair St. Museum)
"Nantucket Historic District Commission Guidebook," 1967
See Architecture

BUNKER-FAMILY

Bunker Family—*I. & M. July 19, 1873*
Origin of the Nantucket Family—*N.H.A. Proc. 1900*
Reunion—*Hist. Nant., Oct. 1959*
"Bunker Genealogy"—*Edward C. Moran Jr., 1942 and 1965*

BURYING GROUNDS

See Cemeteries

C

CALIFORNIA

See Gold Rush

CAMELS

A View of Brant Point and Entrance to Harbor 1820-1842—*a painting by James Walter Folger, 1909, showing Camels (Fair St. Museum)*
Nantucket Marine Camel Co. Report of Committee on Commerce, Feb. 22, 1843 (Crosby Coll.)
Camels—*"The Island of Nantucket", Godfrey, 1882, p. 58*
Camels—*"Nantucket: a History", Douglas-Lithgow, 1914*
The Camels—*"100 Years on Nantucket", I. & M., 1921*
Camels—*Stackpole, N.H.A. Proc. 1940 (with photo)*
Model of Camels (Whaling Museum)

CANES

Boston Post Cane for Oldest Citizen—*I. & M. Nov., 1949 and Boston Herald, Feb. 28, 1969*
Large collection scrimshawed canes (Whaling Museum, Scrimshaw Rm.)
Other collections (Fair St. Museum and private ownership)

CAPAUM

House Lot Map of Capaum Settlement 1665-1680—*N.H.A. Bull. Vol. 2, Bull. 2 and 4*

CARLISLE RECORDINGS

33 Tape Recordings on Nantucket Subjects Made in 1959 by Henry Coffin Carlisle and given to N.H.A.—*Hist. Nant., Apr. 1963*
For list, see Recordings
Henry C. Carlisle, An Interview in "Mining Engineering," Oct. 1963

CARS, HORSE

Horse Cars—*"100 Years on Nantucket", I. & M., 1921*
See Transportation

CARVINGS

Wood Carvings by James Walter Folger (Case 23, 2nd floor Fair St. Museum)

Carved Portrait of Abram Quary by Aletha Macy—*New Bedford Standard Times, Sept. 1, 1951*

Carved Ivory Whales on Plaque, by Aletha Macy (Kynett Memorial Room, Athen.)

CEMETERIES

Card Catalogue of Inscriptions on All Monuments and Grave-Stones in Old North Burying Ground and Newtown Burying Ground—*made in 1897 and 1898 (Filed in Case, Genealogical Rm., Fair St. Museum)*

Gravestone Records—*See List in "Vital Records of Nantucket to 1850" (Athen.)*

The Ancient Burial Ground—*B. Franklin Folger, Nantucket Weekly Mirror, Dec. 6. 1851*

Cemeteries—*"The Island of Nantucket", Godfrey, 1882, p. 60*

Old Nantucket Cemeteries—*N.H.A. Proc. 1904*

Cemeteries—*"Nantucket: a History", Douglas-Lithgow, 1914*

The Old North Burying Ground—*N.H.A. Proc. 1936*

Burial Grounds—*"Nantucket Odyssey", Guba, 1951*

CENSUS

Heads of Mass. Families—*1st Census of the U.S.A. 1790 (Athen.)*

Nantucket Censuses of 1800, 1810, 1820, 1830, 1870, 1880 and 1895, and "Record of deaths from earliest dates they can be collected since the Island of Nantucket was inhabited by the whites". List of deaths beginning Sept., 1834 and list of deaths and where buried, 1826. (micro. Athen.)

Census Book Nantucket 1719-1870 taken from house of Dr. Arthur E. Jenks (Vault, Fair St. Museum)

A Century of Population Growth in the U.S. 1790-1900—*U.S. Bureau of Census, 1909*

CENTENNIAL

"Nantucket's Centennial Celebration 1695-1795-1895"—*Dudley, 1895 (Athen.)*

"100 Years on Nantucket", Centennial Number I. & M. June 23, 1921

CHARACTERS

"Photos of Nantucket Characters by Wyer", Nantucket, 1892

Local Characters—*"Nantucket Scrap Basket", Macy, 1916*

CHARTS

See Maps

CHASE, REUBEN

Reuben Chase—*"Nantucket, the Far-Away Island"—Stevens, 1936*

CHEESE

See Lafayette

CHINA

China—*"Loan Exhibition of Heirlooms", published for Nantucket Cottage Hospital Fete, I. & M. Press, 1935 (Athen.)*

China Collections, Fair Street Museum and 1800 House, N.H.A.

China Pepper Pot Collection (Fair St. Museum)

CHROMOS

See Pictures

CHURCHES

Churches—*Vol. 1 and 2 G.B.G. Scrapbooks (micro. Athen.)*

Second Methodist Church, Sermon Preached 1823 at Dedication of the Chapel—*Maffitt, The Inquirer, Nantucket, 1826*

"Unitarian Belief"—Edes,—*Freeman & Bolles, Boston, 1836*

"Timothy White Papers"—*Dudley, 1898 (Athen.)*

Baptist Church, Nantucket, 3 volumes records from 1839 (In possession Rev. Arthur E. Darby, 3 Howard St., Nantucket)

"The Brotherhood of Thieves"—*Foster, New London, Published by Wm. Bolles, 1843 (Vault, Fair St. Museum)*

"Churches and Pastors"—*Dudley, 1902 (Athen.)*

Congregational Meeting House Floor Plan—*Dudley, N.H.A. Bull., Vol. 1, Bull. 2*

History of the Unitarian Church—*Rev. Meyers, 1902 (Church Files in Vestry, Nantucket)*

The Colonial Church and Nantucket—*Worth, N.H.A. Proc. 1906*

Organizational Papers 2nd Congregational Meeting House Society (Unitarian) —*(In frames on display at Unitarian Church, Nantucket)*

Churches of Nantucket—*"100 Years on Nantucket", I. & M. 1921*

Churches of Nantucket—*Starbuck, "History of Nantucket", 1924*

Universalism in Nantucket—*"The Coffin Saga", Gardner, 1949*

Unitarian Church—*Hist. Nant., Jan. 1965*

Universalism in Nantucket—*Hist. Nant., July, 1966*

Baptist Church—*Hist. Nant., Jan. 1961 and July, 1962*

Old Steeple, Baptist—*Nantucket Town Crier, Dec. 2, 1960*

First Congregational Church in Nantucket, History, Sketch and Catalogue of Members, 1767-1905 (Mrs. Kent King, Nantucket)

Methodist and Unitarian Organs—*Hist. Nant., Apr. 1963 and N.H.A. Proc. 1902.*

Congregational Church, Methodist Church, Unitarian Church—*see Buildings Documented for HABS*

North Church Gets New Steeple—*I. & M. Sept. 12, 1968*

"Steeple Out of Mid-Air"—*Stackpole, Yankee Magazine, Dec. 1968*

A Steeple Comes Back to an Old Church—*Hist. Nant., Jan., 1969*

CIRCUS

Circus at Nantucket—*Framed poster advertising circus at Nantucket in 1847 (Fair St. Museum)*

CLOCKS

Town Clock—*"The Island of Nantucket", Godfrey, 1882, p. 82*

Walter Folger Clock—*N.H.A. Proc. 1920*

Walter Folger Clock—*Hist. Nant. Oct., 1953*

"The Clock That Talks"—*Dr. Will Gardner, 1954*

Tall clock, a gift of Annie Barker Folger, 1928, with works by Thos. Wagstaffe, a London Quaker, and purchased from him by one of the Nantucketers who lodged at his wife's boarding-house on trips abroad (Entrance Hall Athen.)

Grandmother Clock, bequest of Mr. and Mrs. Everett U. Crosby (Whaling Museum)

Other tall clocks at Fair St. Museum, Whaling Museum, 1800 House, Hadwen House-Satler Memorial—*all property of N.H.A.*

Tall clock at Nantucket Cottage Hospital reception room, formerly owned by
Captain James Bunker, c. 1815

CLUBS
See Organizations

COAST GUARD
Awards to Nantucket Men By the Mass. Humane Society—*"Wrecks Around
Nantucket", Gardner, 1877, with added material by Turner and Sayle in edi-
tion of 1954.*
Coast Guard—*Hist. Nant., Jan. 1965 and Jan. 1966*
Mass. Humane Society on Nantucket—*Hist. Nant. Apr. 1966*
Loran C., Station of U.S. Coast Guard—*Barnes, Hist. Nant., Oct. 1962*
See also Lighthouses and Lightships

COATS OF ARMS
Framed Coats of Arms of Nantucket Families (on Walls Fair St. Museum
Library and in Chest at Fair St. Meeting House)

COATUE
Coatue—*Crosby, Hist. Nant., Jan. 1965*
Coatue Through Muskeget—*Vol. 31, G.B.G. Scrapbooks (micro. Athen.)*

CODD, WILLIAM
William Codd—*I. & M. Mar. 16, 1940*

COFFIN FAMILY
Account of Admiral Coffin's Visit to Nantucket in 1829—*(In Files, Fair St.
Museum)*
"Miriam Coffin"—*Hart, 1834*
"The Life of Tristram Coffin"—*Allen Coffin, 1881*
"Trustum and His Grandchildren"—*Worron, 1881*
"The Coffin Family"—*Brown, 1881*
"The Life of Sir Isaac Coffin, Baronet"—*Amory, 1886*
Tristram Coffin—*Family Memoirs of Mrs. George L. Carlisle, 1925 (Crosby
Coll.)*
Sir Isaac Coffin, Bart—*N.H.A. Proc. 1901 and 1932*
"Keziah Coffin"—*N.H.A. Proc. 1939 and 1912*
Captains George F. and Peter F. Coffin—*N.H.A. Proc. 1949*
"The Coffin Saga"—*Gardner, 1949*
Coffin Family Reunion—*Hist. Nant., Oct .1959*
Coffin Ancestral Home—*Hist. Nant., Apr. 1959*
"The Coffin Family"—*Louis Coffin, 1962 (micro. Athen.)*

COMMONS
See Land

CONSERVATION
Conservation—*Hist. Nant., Jan. 1966*
"Selected Resources of the Island of Nantucket", Publication No. 4 Cooperative
Extension Service, Univ. of Mass. cooperating with U.S. Dept. Agriculture,
1967.

COOK-BOOKS, NANTUCKET
"Nantucket Recipes", N.E. Hospital for Women and Children, Rockwell &
Churchill Press, Boston, 1874 (micro. Athen.)
The Centennial Cookbook, 1795-1895—*M.M. Assoc. Publication*
Recipes—*Ladies of North Congregational Church, Nantucket, 1902*
Old Nantucket and 'Sconset Receipts—*Marion Crosby, 1910 (Crosby Coll.)*
Nantucket Receipts—*Inquirer and Mirror, 1915 (micro. Athen.)*
Nantucket Island Cookbook—*Old People's Home, n.d. (micro. Athen.)*

Favorite Cooking Recipes—*Sherburne Chapt. Eastern Star, 1935*
Nantucket Cookbook—*Harmonious Hustlers North Congregational Church, Nantucket, 1943 (micro. Athen.)*
Handwritten Cookbook, n.d. (micro. Athen.)
Grange Cookbook, 1969
"From the Galleys of Nantucket"—*First Congregational Church, Nantucket Island, Mass. 1969*

COURTS OF NANTUCKET
Courts—*Worth, N.H.A. Bull., Vol. 2, Bull. 2*
Courts—*N.H.A. Proc. 1907, p. 30*

CRAFTS
See Industries

CRANBERRIES
See Industries

CREVECOEUR, J. HECTOR ST. JOHN DE
An American Farmer's Letters from Nantucket—*N.H.A. Proc. 1905*
Crévecoeur—*"Nantucket in Print", Crosby, 1946*
"Letters From an American Farmer"—*(Copies of several different editions at Athen., some on microfilm)*

CROOKED RECORD
See Land

CROSBY FAMILY
Crosby Family—*I. & M., July 19, 1873*

CURFEW
See Bell

CUSTOMS
See Sayings and Customs

CUSTOMS HOUSE AT NANTUCKET
Customs House, with List of Collectors—*"100 Years on Nantucket", I. & M. 1921*
Custom House Ledger, 1849 (Whaling Museum)

D

DAUPHIN
Wax Figure of Dauphin (Fair St. Museum)
Wax Image of Dauphin at Nantucket—*"100 Years on Nantucket", I. & M., 1921*
Correspondence re Dauphin (Files, Fair St. Museum)

DECOYS
Old Decoys (Case #9, Fair St. Museum)
Collection of About 70 Old Decoys at Museum—*Hist. Nant. Oct. 1955*

DEEDS
Records of County Deeds from 1659 to date (micro. Reg. Deeds, Nantucket)
Thomas Dongan Patent (In covered box on wall, Reg. Deeds, Nantucket)
Nantucket Patent 1695 (New York State Archives)
"Papers Relating to the Island of Nantucket"—*Hough, 1856*
Deed of 1722, signed by Jethro Coffin (Rare Items File, Fair St. Museum)
Framed Copy of Early Indian Deed (Store-room, Fair St. Museum)
Deed to Island from Mayhew 1641—*Hist. Nant. Jan. 1959*

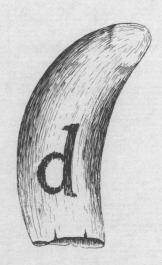

Names of Island in Earliest Deeds—*"Nantucket in Print"*, *Crosby, 1946*
Title From English King—*Worth, N.H.A. Bull. ,Vol. 2, Bull. 1*
Original Lay-Outs on Harbor—*Worth, N.H.A. Bull., Vol. 2, Bull. 4*

DESCRIPTIONS OF NANTUCKET, EARLY

"Letters From an American Farmer"—*Crévecoeur, 1782*
A Topographical Description of Nantucket—*Walter Folger, Mass. Hist. Soc. Coll. 1st Series, Vol. III, 1791*
Account of Journey by Josiah Quincy—*Proc. Mass. Hist. Soc. 2nd Series, Vol. IV, 1801*
Notes on Nantucket—*Rev. James Freeman, Coll. Mass. Hist. Soc. 2nd Series, Vol. III, 1807*
Nantucket—*Joseph Sansom, Port Folio, Philadelphia, 1811*
Description of Nantucket—*Ralph Waldo Emerson, Entry of May 23, 1847, in "Emerson's Journals", published by Houghton, Mifflin & Company, Boston, 1912. See "Nantucket in Print", Crosby, 1946, p. 151.*
"Moby Dick"—*Melville, 1851*
Nantucket—*Scribner's Monthly, August, 1873*
Nantucket—*Frank Leslie's Sunday Magazine, August, 1882*
Island Nantucket—*Brooks, Reprint from The Geographical Review, Sept., 1917*

DISCOVERY OF NANTUCKET

Discovery—*"Nantucket: a History", Douglas-Lithgow, 1914*
Discoverers of Nantucket—*Crosby, N.H.A. Proc. 1943*

DOCUMENTS

Copies of "Declaration of Anti-Slavery Convention"; "The Art of Making Money Plenty" by Dr. Benjamin Franklin 1817; and original document appointing Stephen Hussey Inspector of Revenue, signed by Geo. Washington 1792 (Vault, Fair St. Museum)
Other Important Documents in Rare Items File Fair St. Museum.
Framed Document Printed on Silk 1829: Remonstrance Against Delivering Mail on Sabbath, Report from U.S. Senate Committee (Fair St. Museum)
Quaker Documents (On Walls of Quaker Meeting House, N.H.A.)
Document of "Leave and Permission" for Ship "Ohio", from Ulysses S. Grant, President of the United States, dated July 3, 1875 (On Wall of Pres. Grant Room, Jared Coffin House, Nantucket)
Large box miscellaneous documents (Mrs. Lewis S. Edgarton, Nantucket)
Framed letter to Josiah Coffin, Esq. from the Nantucket Gaol in 1771, written by Thomas Arthur and signed "The King's True and Faithful Prisoner, March 8, 1771" (Mrs. Lewis S. Edgarton, Nantucket)

DONGAN PATENT
See Deeds

DUDLEY, MYRON S.
Myron S. Dudley—*N.H.A. Proc. 1940*

DUNKIRK
Proposal to Transfer Whaling to France—*"History of Nantucket", Obed Macy, 1835*
"The Sea Hunters"—*Stackpole, 1953*
"Nantucket Odyssey"—*Guba, 1951*

DWELLINGS
See Buildings

E

EASTON
George Easton Papers re Sheep Commons, Wills, Land Grants and Purchases, c. 1800 (Vault, Fair St. Museum)

EDUCATION
Outline of Nantucket History Course Given at High School-Grace Brown Gardner, 1943 (micro. Athen.)
Education—*New England Galaxy, June 9, 1826*
See Schools

EIGHTEEN HUNDRED HOUSE
Descriptive pamphlet published by N.H.A.
Interior of 1800 House—*Hist. Nant., July, 1953*

EMBROIDERY
Handmade Articles (Case #8 Fair Street Museum)
Classes With Miss Rivett—*Hist. Nant., July, 1965*
See Samplers

EMERSON, RALPH WALDO
"Emerson's Journals"—*Published by Houghton, Mifflin & Co., Boston, 1912. Entry of May 23, 1847 describes visit to Nantucket*
Emerson's Lectures at Nantucket—*Hist. Nant., Apr. 1957, p. 13-14*

EMIGRATION
"History of Nantucket"—*Obed Macy, 1835*
Settlement of Hudson, N.Y.—*"The Island of Nantucket", Godfrey, 1882, p. 200*
"History of Nantucket", Starbuck, 1924
Emigrations from Nantucket—*"Nantucket Odyssey", Guba, 1951*
"The Sea Hunters", Stackpole, 1953
Emigration from Nantucket to Hudson, N.Y.—*Hist. Nant., Apr. 1968*

ENGLAND—NANTUCKET RELATIONS WITH
"History of Nantucket"—*Obed Macy, 1835*
Nantucket in the Revolution—*The History and Genealogical Register, Boston, 1874-5*
"History of Nantucket", Starbuck, 1924, p. 269 and 389
Nantucket in the Revolution—*Arthur H. Gardner, New England Magazine, Jan., 1905*
"William Rotch of Nantucket"—*Stackpole, The Newcomen Soc. of North America, 1950*

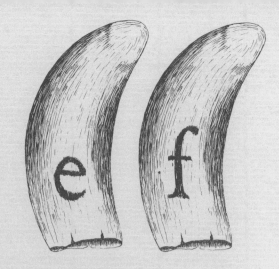

Hospital Fete 1929—*Souvenir No., I & M., Aug. 17, 1929 (Crosby Coll.)*

FAMILY TREES

Family Trees of Nantucket Families, including Cartwright, Coffin, Folger and Myrick (Framed Paintings, 2nd Floor Walls Fair St. Museum)

FANNING, KEZIA COFFIN

Kezia Coffin Fanning—*"History of Nantucket", Starbuck, 1924, p. 205*
See Manuscripts
See Portraits

FARMS AND FARMING

Farming—*Vol. 3 G.B.G. Scrapbooks (micro. Athen.)*
Nantucket Farms (with map)—*N.H.A. Proc. 1947 and I. & M. Aug. 9, 1947*
Farming—*"Letters From an American Farmer", Crévecoeur, 1782, p. 9 and 10*
Agriculture—*"Nantucket: a History", Douglas-Lithgow, 1914*
Display of Old Farming Implements (Basement Fair St. Museum)

FAWCETT, GEORGE

George Fawcett—*Biography by Dr. Wm. E. Gardner (micro. Athen.)*
See Actors on Nantucket

FIRES AT NANTUCKET

Fire Watch Established—*Records of Selectmen, Nantucket, Apr. 6, 1801 (Town Clerk's Office, Nantucket)*
Fire of 1836 Pictures (In Portfolio, Fair St. Museum and in office of Congdon & Coleman, Nantucket)
Fire of 1838—*I. & M., Jan. 2, 1897*
Maps and Pictures of 1838 and 1846 Fires (Fair St. Museum; Whaling Museum and Athen.)
Great Fire at Nantucket—*New York Daily Tribune July 16 and July 23, 1846*
Fire Supplement with History of Dept. and Fires—*I. & M., 1916*
History of Nantucket Fire Dept.—*"100 Years on Nantucket", I. & M. 1921*
Great Fire Hit Nantucket Hard—*"100 Years on Nantucket", I. & M. 1921*
Eighty-Fifth Anniversary of Nantucket's "Great Fire"—*I. & M. July 11, 1931*
Great Fire of 1846—*Stackpole, N.H.A. Proc. 1946*
Fire Department—*Bartlett, Hist. Nant., Jan. 1959*
Fire of Sun., July 24, 1949—*I. & M. Supplement, Aug. 6, 1949*
Gardner Street Fire Hose Cart House—*Hist. Nant. Oct. 1963*
Fire Buckets on Display—*(Fair St. Museum and 1800 House N.H.A.)*
Fire Engines on Display—*(Fair St. Museum)*
Fire Trumpet and Staff Used in Fire of 1836—*(Fair St. Museum)*

FISH AND FISHERIES

Fishing—*Vol. 12 G.B.G. Scrapbooks (micro. Athen.)*
Cod Fishing—*"Letters From an American Farmer", Crévecoeur, 1782, p. 125*
Report on Cod and Whale Fisheries—*U.S. Sec. of State, 1791 (Athen.)*
Blue Fish—*Zaccheus Macy, Mass. Hist. Soc. Coll., 1st Series, Vol. III, 1792*
Blackfish—*The Daily Graphic, New York, July 10, 1874*
Blackfish—*Frank Leslie's Illustrated Newspaper, Sept. 13, 1879*
Blue Fishing at Nantucket (with illustration)—*Frank Leslie's Illustrated Newspaper, Aug. 30, 1879*
The Fisheries and Fishing Industries of the U.S.—*Washington Printing Office, 1887 (Athen.)*
Report of Committee on Subject of Fisheries—*U.S. Committee of Fish and Fisheries, 1873 (Athen.)*
"A History of the New England Fisheries"—*R. McFarland, Philadelphia, 1911*
Quahaug War in Nantucket Sound—*Science Magazine, Aug. 18, 1916*
The 1914 Clam Bed Outside Jetties—*Recording by King, 1959 (N.H.A.)*
Fish, Shellfish and Lobsters—*Recording by McCleave and King, 1959 (N.H.A.)*
"Down to the Sea for Fish"—*Reynolds Printing, New Bedford, 1939*

Harbor Scallop Survey of 1933—*I. and M., Apr. 3, 1948*
Government of Fisheries of the Great Ponds of Nantucket—*Hist. Nant.,
    Apr. 1965*
"The Outer Lands"—*Sterling, 1967*
See Ponds

FISH HOUSES

Fish Houses as a Group—*North and South Sides Old South Wharf, documented
    1965 for H.A.B.S. (Athen. and Lib. Cong.)*

FISH LOTS

Fish Lot Shares as Laid Out in 1717—*Proprietor's Book of Plans #1, p. 2
    (Registry Deeds, Nantucket)*
Fish Lot Shares, map—*"History of Nantucket", Starbuck, 1924*

FLAGS

United States 24 star flag, handmade—*(Mrs. Lewis S. Edgarton, Nantucket)*
Private Signal Flag of Captain Henry F. Coffin—*(Mrs. Lewis S. Edgarton,
    Nantucket)*
Macy Ship Signals—*(Fair St. Museum)*
Signal Flags of Nantucket Ships—*(Framed, at Fair St. Museum)*
Signal Flags—*"The Story of Yankee Whaling", Shapiro & Stackpole, 1959*

FLORA AND FAUNA

Plants—*Vol. 3 G.B.G. Scrapbooks (micro. Athen.)*
"Catalogue of Plants Growing Without Cultivation at Nantucket"—*Mrs. Maria
    L. Owen, 1888 (M.M. Library) (List also appears on p. 39 "The Island of
    Nantucket", Godfrey, 1882.)*
"Ferns and Flowering Plants of Nantucket"—*Bicknell, Bull. Torrey Botanical
    Club, 1908-1919 (M.M. Library)*
"Nantucket, a Brief Sketch of its Physiography and Botany"—*Sara Winthrop
    Smith, 1901 (Crosby Coll.)*
"Nantucket Wild Flowers"—*Albertson, 1921*
"A Grain of Mustard Seed"—*Shurrocks, 1958*
The Nantucket Flora—*"Nantucket: a History", Douglas-Lithgow, 1914*
"Boggy Solitudes of Nantucket"—*Wilson, 1908*
Hidden Forest—*"Nantucket, the Far-Away Island", Stevens, 1936*
"The Outer Lands"—*Sterling, 1967*
"Native and Naturalized Plants of Nantucket"—*MacKeever, 1968*
"Poison Ivy and Ragweed"—*Civic League of Nantucket, 1952*
Mosses and Liverworts of Nantucket—*Rice, 1942 (M.M. Library)*
Nantucket Forests—*N.H.A. Proc. 1935, p. 19-27*
Scotch Broom, Gorse, Heather and English Ivy—*N.H.A. Proc. 1920*
Old Nantucket Gardens—*N.H.A. Proc. 1920*
Elm Trees on Main Street—*N.H.A. Proc. 1920*
Peat—*N.H.A. Proc. 1922, p. 58*
Napoleon Willows—*N.H.A. Proc. 1920, p. 42; 1924, p. 14; and Hist. Nant.
    Apr. 1961*
Nantucket Heather—*Hist. Nant., Oct. 1955*
Fungi of Nantucket—*Guba, 1937, 1939 and 1942 (M.M. Publications)*
Nantucket Moors—*I. & M. Oct. 5, 1940*
Deer on Nantucket—*"Nantucket, the Far-Away Island", Stevens, 1936, p. 268*
Deer on Nantucket—*"Argument Settlers", Turner, 1966, p. 107 and 127*
Prairie Chickens—*"Argument Settlers", Turner, 1966, p. 62*
Prairie Dogs—*"Argument Settlers", Turner, 1966, p. 69*
See Insects for Spiders and Moths

FOLGER FAMILY

Folger Family—*I. & M. July 19, 1873*
The Folgers of Old Capaum—*N.H.A. Proc. 1935, p. 16*
Nantucket Folgers in Ohio—*N.H.A. Proc. 1944*

Storm Supplement, I. and M., Feb. 2, 1889
Ice Embargo—*I. and M. Supplement, Mar. 2, 1912*
Freeze-Up Supplement, I. and M., Mar. 10, 1934
Freeze-Ups—*Hist. Nant., Apr. 1957*

FRIENDS
See Quakers

G

GAOL
The Old Nantucket Gaol—*Stackpole, N.H.A. Publication, n.d.*
Gaol and Building—*Records Nantucket Town Meetings Dec. 29, 1804 and Apr. 22, 1805 (Town Clerk's Office, Nantucket)*
Old Gaol—*Building Documented for H.A.B.S. 1935 (Lib. Cong.)*

GALLERIES, KENNETH TAYLOR
See Foundation

GARDENS
Old Nantucket Gardens—*N.H.A. Proc. 1920*

GARDNER, GRACE BROWN
62 Scrapbooks on Nantucket subjects. See Scrapbooks

GARDNER FAMILY
Very old Gardner Family Bible, 1762 (Mrs. Lewis S. Edgarton, Nantucket)
Quaker Wedding Certificate of Matthew Gardner and Susanna Paddock
   (Mrs. Lewis S. Edgarton, Nantucket)
"Sketch-Book" (log-book) of George W. Gardner (micro. Athen.)
Arthur H. Gardner—*N.H.A. Proc. 1924, p. 28*
John Gardner—*"History of Nantucket", Starbuck, 1924*
John Gardner—*"The Triumphant Captain John", Gardner, 1958*
"Anna Gardner, The Quaker School Marm"—*The Virginia Magazine of History and Biography, Oct. 1953*
Dr. William E. Gardner—*Bound copy of biography (micro. Athen.)*

GAYER, WILLIAM
William Gayer and His Descendants—*N.H.A. Proc. 1922, p. 38*

GENEALOGY

Vital Statistics—*5 volumes Births, Marriages and Deaths at Nantucket to the Year 1850, as prepared by New England Historic Genealogical Society, Boston, 1925 (Athen.)*

Nantucket Vital Statistics (Records Town Clerk Nantucket)

Pollard Papers—*4 large folio volumes prepared by Miss Eliza Pollard (micro. Athen.)*

Sanford Papers—*Prepared by Frederick C. Sanford's sister (micro. Athen.)*

Barney Records—*7 manuscript volumes by Mrs. Eliza Barney (McCleary Case, Fair St. Museum)*

Records compiled by George & Caleb Bunker—*The New England Historical and Genealogical Register, Vol. 51*

The Genealogists of Nantucket—*Allen, Magazine of New England History II, 1892*

"One Hundred and Sixty Allied Families"—*Austin, 1893 (Fair St. Museum)*

William C. Folger—*10 volumes of records (Fair St. Museum)*

"Coffin Family"—*Louis Coffin, 1962*

Genealogical Scrapbook G.B.G. (micro. Athen.)

Historical Records Compiled by George Howland Folger, 1870 (Fair St. Museum)

Family Trees of Nantucket Families Including Cartwright, Folger, Mitchell, Myrick, Macy (Fair St. Museum)

Genealogical Records (Library, Fair St. Museum)

See Family Names

GEOLOGY

Survey of Island of Nantucket—*Secretary of War, Washington, 1828 (Crosby Coll.)*

Geology of Nantucket—*"The Island of Nantucket", Godfrey, 1882, p. 48*

Geology of the Island of Nantucket—*Shaler, U.S. Dept. Interior, Bull. #43, 1889 (Crosby Coll.)*

Man and the Glacial Period—*Wright, 1892 (Athen.)*

Nantucket, a Moranial Island—*Curtis & Woodworth, Univ. of Chicago, 1899*

Changes in Ocean Shore-Lines of Nantucket Island—*Appendix No. 6, Report for 1892, U.S. Coast and Geodetic Survey, Washington, 1893*

Nantucket Shorelines II—*Gulliver, Bull. of Geological Soc., Nov. 1904*

Glacial History of Nantucket and Cape Cod—*Wilson, London, 1906 (Athen.)*

Geology & Physiography of the Island—*"Nantucket, a History", Douglas-Lithgow, 1914*

Soil Survey of Dukes and Nantucket Counties, Mass.—*Latimer, U.S. Dept. Agriculture, No. 28, Series 1925*

Geography and Geology of the Region, including Nantucket—*Woodworth and Wigglesworth, Cambridge, Mass., 1934 (Athen.)*

"These Fragile Outposts"—*Chamberlain, 1964*

Glacial Formation of Nantucket—*Hist. Nant., Apr. 1969*

GILPATRICK

Dr. Roy Hawkes Gilpatrick—*Biography (micro. Athen.)*

GLASS

Rare Sandwich Glass and Other Glass (Fair St. Museum)

GLOBE

See Mutiny

GOLD RUSH

"A List of Persons from Nantucket Now in California"—*Published by Jethro C. Brock, Nantucket, Jan. 1, 1850 (micro. Athen)*

Six Months in the Gold Mines"—*Buffum, 1850 (Athen.)*

The California Fever — *"The Island of Nantucket", Godfrey, 1882 p. 206*

"A Pioneer Voyage to California and Round the World on Ship Alhambra"—

Coffin, 1908 (*Grace Brown Gardner, Nantucket*)
Nantucket Forty-Niners—*Winslow, Hist. Nant., Jan. 1956*
Argonauts of '49—*Howe, c. 1920*
Writing Recently Discovered on Wall of Attic at 52 Centre St., Nantucket, "Aug. 16, 1849. Elisha Doan, Uriah Russell, Christopher Capen, John B. Coffin, left this morning for California. May they be preserved—"

GOLF CLUBS

Golf Clubs—*Vol. 42, G.B.G. Scrapbooks (micro. Athen.)*
Golf Clubs—*N.H.A. Proc. 1920, p. 33*

GRANT

Pres. Ulysses S. Grant's Visit to Nantucket—*N.H.A. Proc. 1947*
Captain George A. Grant—*N.H.A. Proc. 1941*

GRAVELLY ISLANDS

Gravelly Islands—*Worth N.H.A. Bull., Vol. 2, Bull. 1*

GRAVESTONE RECORDS

See Cemeteries

GULF STREAM

Gulf Stream—*Dr. Benjamin Franklin, American Museum, Phila., Pa., 1789, p. 213*
The Real Gulf Stream—*Dr. I. I. Hayes, The Galaxy, Jan. 1872*
"The Gulf Stream"—*"Works of Benjamin Franklin", Vol. iii, pp. 353-364*
Recent Discoveries Concerning the Gulf Stream—*Pillsbury, Feb. 1892 (Athen.)*
Where is Franklin's First Chart of Gulf Stream?—*Bache, American Philosophical Society, Vol. LXXVI, No. 5, 1936*
The Gulf Stream—*Nantucket Foundation Inc. Bull. #49-C*

H

HADWEN HOUSE—SATLER MEMORIAL

Hadwen House—*Satler Memorial—Leaflet published by N.H.A.*
Hadwen House—*Hist. Nant., July, 1964*
96 Main Street—*Building Documented for H.A.B.S. (Athen.)*

HALIFAX

See Nova Scotia

HALLS, EARLY

Atheneum Hall, Atlantic Hall, Wendell's Hall, Institute Hall, Pantheon Hall, Sherburne Hall, North Hall—*"The Island of Nantucket", Godfrey, 1882*
Pantheon Hall—*N.H.A. Proc. 1919, p. 27*
Atlantic Hall—*N.H.A. Proc. 1923, p. 55*
Wendell's Hall—*N.H.A. Proc. 1923, p. 56*

HANAFORD, PHEBE ANN (COFFIN)

Phebe Hanaford—"Women of Nantucket"—*N.H.A. Proc. 1912*
Mrs. Hanaford—*N.H.A. Proc. 1929*

HARBOR

Survey of Harbour in the Island of Nantucket—*U.S. Committee of Commerce & Manufactures, 1803 (micro. Athen.)*
An Estimate of Building Two Piers for the Harbor of Nantucket—*U.S. Secretary of Treasury, 1803 (micro. Athen.)*
Survey of Nantucket Harbor—*Report of U.S. Sec. of War, Washington, 1828*
Survey of Nantucket Harbor—*Van Ingen, I. & M., Dec. 25, 1875*
Bar, Jetty & Harbor—*"The Island of Nantucket", Godfrey, 1882*
Massachusetts Harbour Commission—*7th Annual Report, Jan., 1878*
Report on Nantucket Harbour—*U.S. Army Corps of Engineers, Washington, 1941*

HAULOVER

Map of the Haulover Opening Before Closing—*J. H. Robinson, 1908 (Fair St. Museum)*
Haulover—*"100 Years on Nantucket", I. & M., 1921*
Haulover—*"Nantucket, the Far-Away Island", Stevens, 1936*
Nantucket's Haulover—*Report by Wm. F. Jones, I. & M. Apr. 2, 1938*
The Haulover Opening—*Recording by Bunt Mackay, 1959 (N.H.A.)*
Haulover—*"Argument Settlers", Turner, 1966, p. 65*
Haulover—*Hist. Nant., Apr. 1967*

HEALTH

See Epidemics

HEART

Heart of Dr. Winslow—*N.H.A. Proc. 1948*
Heart of Dr. Winslow—*Hist. Nant. Oct. 1963*

HISTORIC AMERICAN BUILDINGS SURVEY

List of Measured Drawings, Photographs and Written Historical Documentation of Historic American Buildings—*Compiled by Historic American Buildings Survey, National Park Service, Department of the Interior, Washington, D.C. (Library Congress)*

HISTORIC DISTRICTS

The Nantucket Historic Districts Commission—*Jones, Hist. Nant., Apr. 1956*
Annual Report 1959 of Historic Districts Commission (Town Clerk's Office, Nantucket)
Annual Report 1965 of Historic Districts Commission (Town Clerk's Office, Nantucket)
"Nantucket Historic Districts Guidebook", Poets Corner Press, Nantucket, 1967

HISTORIC NANTUCKET

Historic Nantucket—Quarterly Publication of N.H.A.—*1st issue July, 1953*

HISTORICAL ASSOCIATION

Beginning of Association—*N.H.A. Proc. 1934*
Historical Assoc.—*Vol. 16 through 19, G.B.G. Scrapbooks (micro. Athen.)*

Nantucket Historical Association, Centennial Catalogue, 1895.
For information on the following exhibits, see name of each:
Whaling Museum; 1800 House; Fair St. Museum; Friends Meeting House;
   Hadwen House-Satler Memorial; Old Mill; Old Gaol; Fire Hose Cart House;
   Oldest House; 'Sconset Pump; Folger-Franklin Memorial.

HISTORY OF NANTUCKET

History Course for High School—*Outline by Grace Brown Gardner*
   (micro. Athen.)
Henry Coffin Carlisle's History Recording Project—*Hist. Nant. Apr. 1963.*
   Also see Recordings.
"The History of Nantucket"—*Obed Macy, 1835*
"Nantucket While Under the Colony of New York"—*Hough, 1856*
"The Island of Nantucket"—*Godfrey, 1882*
"History of Nantucket"—*Alexander Starbuck, 1924 and 1969*
"Nantucket: a History"—*Douglas-Lithgow, 1914*
"The Story of Old Nantucket"—*Macy, 1915*
"The Glacier's Gift"—*Folger, 1911*
"The Nantucket Scrap Basket"—*Macy, 1916*
"Brief Historical Data"—*Farnham, 1915*
"Nantucket, the Far-Away Island"—*Stevens, 1936*
"An Island Patchwork"—*Early, 1941*
"Nantucket Odyssey"—*Guba, 1951 and 1965*
"Argument Settlers"—*Turner, 1917 through 1966*
Nantucket History—*Hist. Nant. July, 1957*
Nantucket's 300 Years, a Brief History—*I. & M. Supplement, 1959*

HORSE CARS

Horse Cars—*"Argument Settlers", Turner, 1966, p. 60. Photo p. 96*

HOSPITAL

Hospital—*Vol. 14 G.B.G. Scrapbooks (micro. Athen.)*
Mass Meeting for Nantucket Cottage Hospital—*I. & M. Aug. 12, 1911*
History of Nantucket Cottage Hospital—*Stackpole, I. & M. Jan. 1941*
New Cottage Hospital—*Hist. Nant., Oct. 1957*
"While You're On the Ways"—*Primer for Patients—Nant. Cottage Hospital, 1957*
"Aunt Dorcas' Change of Heart"—*Waller, 1913 (Athen.)*
Loan Exhibition of Heirlooms Catalogue—*Hospital Committee 1935*
Fete pamphlets, including 1921; 1923; 1925; 1935; 1959; 1961. (Crosby Coll.)
Small Pox Hospital at Gravelly Islands—*Worth N.H.A. Bull., Vol. 2, Bull. 1*

HOTELS

Hotels—*Vol. 5, G.B.G. Scrapbooks (micro. Athen.)*
Ocean House—*Vol. 1 & 2, G.B.G. Scrapbooks (micro. Athen.)*

HOUSE OF CORRECTION

House of Correction Razed—*Hist. Nant., Jan. 1954*
See Gaol

HOUSES

See Buildings

HUDSON, N. Y.

See Emigrations

HUGUENOTS

Our Debt to the Huguenots—*N.H.A. Proc. 1910, p. 43-49*

HUMANE SOCIETY

See Coast Guard

HUMOR

Humor of Nantucket—*N.H.A. Proc. 1904*
Humor in Nantucket—*Recording by Will Gardner 1959 (N.H.A.)*

HUNTING

Plover and Migratory Bird Shooting at Nantucket—*Barlow, 1884*
    (M.M. Assoc. Library)
"Shooting Stands of Eastern Massachusetts"—*Phillips, 1929*
"Shooting Journal", 1865-1922—*Mackay, 1929*
Harriers on Nantucket—*The Spur, July, 1938*
Hunting the Hare—*Polo Magazine, n.d. (Crosby Coll.)*

HURRICANES

See Storms

HUSSEY FAMILY

Husseys at Dorking, England—*Hist. Nant. Apr. 1959*
Hussey Family Reunion—*Hist. Nant. Oct. 1959*

I

ICE

See Freeze-Ups
See Industries

INDIANS

Indians—*Vol. 20 G.B.G. Scrapbooks (micro. Athen.)*
Praying Indians—*Gookin's Historical Collections, 1674 (reprinted in*
    "Nantucket in Print", Crosby, 1946)
An Account of an Extraordinary Disease Among Indians in Islands of Nantucket
    and Marthas Vineyard—*Letter from Andrew Oliver to Mr. Mauduit, Oct. 26,*
    1764 (Crosby Coll.)
Letters Relating to the Sickness of the Indians at Nantucket in 1763
    (Fair St. Museum)
Indian Names—Zaccheus Macy—*Mass. Hist. Soc. 1792*
Indian Tribes—*Gookins, Mass. Hist. Soc. 1st Series, Vol. 1, 1792*
Churches & Population—*Macy, Mass. Hist. Soc. 1st Series, Vol. III, 1792*
Indian Deeds (In Safe, Fair St. Museum)
Deed Book #1 (Registry Deeds, Nantucket)
Indian Churches—John Eliot—*Mass. Hist. Soc. Coll. 1st Series, Vol. X, 1809*
The Nantucket Indian—*Crévecoeur, The Magazine of American History,*
    June, 1878
Indians—*Worth, N.H.A. Bull., Vol. 2, Bull. 3*
Indian Names—*Worth, N.H.A. Vol. 2, Bull. 6*
Indian Place Names of New England—*Huden, Museum of the American Indian,*
    Vol. 18, 1962, p. 135
The Squam Pond Indian Site—*Bullen & Brooks, Bull. Mass. Archaeological Soc.,*
    Andover, Mass., Vol. 8, No. 4, 1947 and Vol. 10, No. 4, 1949
Original Deed From Indians to Edward Starbuck—*N.H.A. Proc. 1917*
Framed Copy Early Indian Deed (Store-Room, Fair St. Museum)
Tashma's Door-Stone—*N.H.A. Proc. 1917 (frontispiece)*
"Nantucket Indians"—*Douglas-Lithgow, 1911*
Indian Place-Names; The Aborigines—*"Nantucket: a History",*
    Douglas-Lithgow, 1914
The Dark Tenant of the Wild—*"Glacier's Gift", Wilson, 1911*
The Indians of Nantucket—*"100 Years on Nantucket", I. & M. 1921*
Indian Legends—*"Nantucket in Print", Crosby, 1946*
Indian Legends—*"Nantucket: a History", Douglas-Lithgow, 1914*

"Other Indian Events of New England"—*Forbes, State Street Trust Co., 1941*
Nantucket Indians Under Mayhew—*"Nantucket Odyssey", Guba, 1951*
Plague Among Indians—*I. & M. Sept. 14, 1929*
Indian Relics, Bones, Skulls, etc. (Case #3 Fair St. Museum)
Dorcas Honorable—*Photo made from daguerrotype of 1844, with biography*
  (Fair St. Museum)
Areas Occupied by Indian Tribes (Shown on Ewer Map, Nantucket, 1869)
See Artifacts
See Quary, Abram

INDUSTRIES IN NANTUCKET

For complete list of publications containing references to the following
  industries, see Historic Nantucket, April, 1957.
  Baskets, Lightship
  Blacksmiths
  Brass Foundry
  Brick Works
  Brush and Bellows Factory
  Candle Factories
  Cattle, Beef
  Clocks and Navigational Instruments
  Coats, Alpaca
  Codfishing
  Cooperage Works
  Cordage Works
  Cranberries
  Duck
  Farming
  Grapes
  Harnesses
  Ice Manufacture
  Iron Works
  Leather Tanneries
  Linen Dusters
  Mills
  Oil Refineries
  Oysters
  Pump and Block Making
  Rope Walks
  Rum Distillery
  Sail Lofts
  Salt Works
  Scallops

Sheep
Ship Building
Shoe Manufacturing
Silkworms
Silversmiths
Stockings
Straw Factory
Spars
Tinsmiths
Twine Plants
Weaving Rag Carpets
Whalebone
Windmills
Woolen Factory
Also see N.H.A. Proc. 1898: 1899: 1920; 1916; 1926 and 1936.

Industries—*Hist. Nant., Jan. 1966*
Manufactures of Nantucket—*"100 Years on Nantucket", I. & M., 1921*
Business People of Nantucket Prior to Fire of 1846—*I. & M. "100 Years on Nantucket", 1921*
Duck Factory—*Hist. Nant., Apr. 1958*
Lightship Baskets—*Recording by Reyes, 1959 (N.H.A.)*
Lightship Baskets—*"Books & Baskets", Crosby, 1940*
Nest of 8 Lightship Baskets made by Capt. James Wyer (Fair St. Mus.)
Nest of Lightship Baskets Made on South Shoal Lightship and given to Capt. Henry P. Coffin for bringing help when supplies ran low (Mrs. Lewis S. Edgarton, Nantucket)
Nantucket Lightship Baskets—*Hist. Nant., Jan. 1969*
Materials Used in Making Baskets (Case #25, 2nd floor, Fair St. Museum)

INSECTS

The Pine Moth of Nantucket—*Scudder, 1883*
A List of the Insect Fauna of Nantucket—*Johnson, 1930 (Athen.)*
Spiders of Nantucket—*Emerton (M.M. Assoc. Library)—1930*
Pinus Thumbergii on Nantucket—*Jones, National Horticultural Magazine, Oct. 1930*
Pinus Thumbergii—*Littlefield, Journal of Forestry, July, 1942*
The Lepidoptera of Nantucket—*Kimball, 1943 (M.M. Assoc. Library)*

J

JAIL
See Gaol

JARED COFFIN HOUSE
See Ocean House

JETHRO COFFIN HOUSE
See Oldest House

JETTIES AND NANTUCKET BAR
Jetties—*"Nantucket: a History", Douglas-Lithgow, 1914*
The Jetties—*"100 Years on Nantucket", I & M. 1921*
Jetties—*Stackpole, N.H.A. Proc. 1940 (with photos)*
See Harbor

JOHNSON, EASTMAN
See Artists

JONES, JOHN PAUL

"History of American Whale Fishery"—*Starbuck, 1878*
John Paul Jones and His Nantucket Fighters—*N.H.A. Proc. 1901 & 1907*
John Paul Jones and His Nantucket Sea Fighters—*Stackpole, N.H.A. Proc. 1936, p. 20-27*

JOURNALS

See Logbooks
An Astronomical Diary or Almanack—*Nathaniel Ames, 1751-1770 (micro. Athen.)*
David Greene's Journal, 1787-1793 (micro. Athen.)
Island Reminiscences—*George F. Worth, n.d. (micro. Athen.)*
Marine Journal, Union Office, 1804-1805 (micro. Athen.)
Notebook of Annie Barker Folger re Distinguished Nantucketers, 1931 (micro. Athen.)
Mrs. Ricketson's Whaling Journal 1871-1874 (micro. Athen.)
Logbook of M. S. Dudley (Fair St. Museum)
Journal of Cruise in U.S. Frigate Essex 1812-1814 (Fair St. Museum)
Whaling Voyage Journal, Ship Dauphin (poetry) (Fair St. Museum)
Journal of William M. Davis on Ship Chelsea 1834-1836 (Fair St. Museum)
Grandmother's Diary of Trip to West Coast—*G.B.G. Scrapbooks, (micro. Athen.)*
Diaries of W. H. Macy and Others (Diary Box, in Safe, Fair St. Museum)
Journal of William B. Starbuck, Quaise, 1870-1873 (micro. Athen.)
5 Old Ledgers of Sweet and Starbuck 1868 (2nd floor storeroom, Fair St. Museum)
William H. Waitt Account Books, 1841-1855 (2nd floor Storeroom, Fair St. Museum)

JOY FAMILY

Moses Joy Jr.—*Biography by Dr. Wm. E. Gardner (micro. Athen.)*
Descendants of Benjamin Cartwright Joy Jr. and the Nantucket Joy Family—*Edward J. Joy, 1940 (Athen.)*

L

LAFAYETTE

The Lafayette Cheese Letter—*"Letters From an American Farmer"—Crévecoeur, French ed. 1787, p. 384, Translation in "Nantucket in Print", Crosby, 1946*
A Cheese for Lafayette—*New Plymouth Newspapers, Sept. 27, 1786*
A Cheese for Lafayette—*I. & M., July 3, 1969 (advertisement)*

LAND

Land—*Vol. 8, G.B.G. Scrapbooks (micro. Athen.)*
"Copy of Records of Common and Undivided Lands for a Period of 40 Years"
—*Town of Nantucket, 1938 (Town Clerk's Office)*
Common and Undivided Lands of Nantucket—*Opinion of Hon. S. S. Wilde, New
Bedford Standard Times, 1851*
Nantucket Lands and Land Owners—*Worth, N.H.A. Bull., Vol. 2, Bull. 1-7*
Sheep Commons and the Proprietary—*Worth, N.H.A. Bull., Vol. 2, Bull. 4*
Speculations in Land—*Worth, N.H.A. Bull., Vol. 2, Bull. 4*
Sheep Commons and Taxation—*I. & M., Aug. 8, 1885*
Common and Undivided Lands of Nantucket—*I. & M. Apr. 11, 1903*
Land Ownership—*C. C. Coffin, "Selected Resources of the Island of Nantucket",
Univ. of Mass., 1967*
Development of Nantucket Land—*C. C. Coffin, I & M., Apr. 20, 1957*
Land Booms—*"Argument Settlers", Turner, 1966, pp. 46, 47, 48*
Land Booms—*Vol. 8, G.B.G. Scrapbooks (micro. Athen.)*
Sherburne Bluffs, Nantucket, Plans for Development of Land Along North
Shore (Rare Book Room, Boston Public Library)
The Common and Undivided Lands of Nantucket—*Lowenthal, The
Geographical Review, Vol. XLVI, No. 3, 1956*
The Land Question—*"Nantucket Odyssey", Guba, 1951*
"A Nest of Love Disturbed", I. & M. Feb. 9, 1935. Reprint of pamphlet
published in 1811
Posting of Land at Nantucket—*Bull. #3 Nantucket Foundation Inc. 1940*
Proprietors, Past and Present—*Stackpole, I. & M., June 29, 1940*
Crooked Record—*"Nantucket Centennial Celebration"—Myron Samuel Dudley,
1895, p. 22*
"Some of Our Island is Missing"—*Lawyer Title News, Aug. 1968*

LEGENDS

Indian Legend Re Discovery Nantucket and Origin of Fog—*Alden, Mass. Hist.
Soc. Coll., 1st Series, Vol. V, 1797*
The Tradition of the Taumhods—*Jenks, Galaxy Magazine, Feb. 2, 1827*
Legends of Nantucket—*I. & M., Feb. 28, 1829*
"A Book of New England Legends and Folk Lore"—*Drake, 1883 (Athen)*
Legends—*"Nantucket: a History", Douglas-Lithgow, 1914*
Legends—*"Nantucket Odyssey", Guba, 1951*
Indian Legends—*"Nantucket in Print", Crosby, 1946*

LEGISLATORS

List of Nantucket's Legislators Since 1780—*"100 Years on Nantucket", I. & M.,
1921*

LIGHTHOUSES AND LIGHTSHIPS

Lighthouses and Lightships—*Vol. 9 G.B.G. Scrapbooks (micro. Athen)*
The Life-Saving Service on Nantucket—*"100 Years on Nantucket", I. & M. 1921*
Lifesaving—*Recording by B. Chester Pease, Hist. Nant., Jan. 1959 (N.H.A.)*
Lifesaving—*Stackpole, I. & M. Dec. 25, 1943*
Lifesaving Service and Wrecks—*"Nantucket: a History", Douglas-Lithgow, 1914*
Life on the South Shoal Lightship—*Kobbé, Century Magazine, Aug. 1891*
South Shoal Lightship Lost in 1905—*Colliers, Dec. 30, 1905 and New Bedford
Standard-Times, Dec. 18, 1955*
Nantucket South Shoals Station—*I. & M., May 16, 1931*
Nantucket Lightship—*New York Times, Mar. 16, 1953*
Cross Rip Lightship—*Hist. Nant., Oct., 1963*
The Sinking of the Nantucket Lightship—*Recording by Tripp, 1959 (N.H.A.)*
Nantucket Lighthouses—*Hist. Nant., July, 1956*
Nantucket Lighthouses—*N.H.A. Proc. 1933, p. 20-22*
Lighthouses and Lightships of Nantucket—*"100 Years on Nantucket", I. & M.
1921*

"Famous New England Lighthouses"—*Snow, 1945*
Brant Point Lighthouse—*"Nantucket: a History", Douglas-Lithgow, 1914*
Lights Far Out to Sea—*"Glacier's Gift", Wilson, 1911*
The Saga of Sankaty—*Stackpole, I. & M., Dec. 25, 1943 and N.H.A. Proc. 1950*
Lenses Installed in Sankaty Light in 1851 now in Whaling Museum—*"The Nantucket Whaling Museum", Nelson, 1955*

LIGHTSHIP BASKETS
See Industries

LOGBOOKS
Fine Collection of approx. 300 Logbooks, Indexed, Numbered and on Microfilm (Whaling Museum)
Over 50 Logbooks and Journals. including Rand Collection on Permanent Loan (micro. Athen.)
Many additional Logbooks privately owned on Nantucket.
Material on Whaling, with Census of Logs—*T. H. Jenkins, British Museum, c. 1949*
"Log of Ship Alexander"—*Hist. Nant., Apr. 1959*
See Journals

LOOMS
Carpet Loom and Small Hand Loom—*(1800 House, N.H.A.)*

LORAN STATION
See Coast Guard

M

MACY FAMILY
Exiles—*"The North Star", Whittier, 1840*
Genealogy of the Macy Family 1635-1868—*Silvanus J. Macy (Athen.)*
Macy Family—*I. & M. July 19, 1873*
William F. Macy—*N.H.A. Proc. 1936 and 1945*
Wendell Macy Paintings—*Hist. Nant., Oct. 1958*
Visiting Our Ancestral Homes—*Hist. Nant. Apr. 1959*
Reunion—*Hist. Nant. Oct. 1959*
"R. H. Macy, The Indomitable"—*Johnson, 1964*
See Carvings by Aletha Macy

MADAKET

Maddaket—*"The Island of Nantucket", Godfrey, 1882, p. 218*
Madaket—*N.H.A. Proc. 1937*
Madaket—*"Nantucket Odyssey", Guba, 1951*
Early Madaket—*Recording by Ray & Runk, 1959 (Fair St. Museum)*
Madaket—*Vol. 31, G.B.G. Scrapbooks (micro. Athen.)*
Mattaket and Great Neck 1821—*Proprietors' Book of Plans #1, p. 45 (Registry Deeds, Nantucket)*
Madaket Development—*"Argument Settlers", Turner, 1966, p. 47*

MANUFACTURERS OF NANTUCKET

See Industries

MANUSCRIPTS, OLD

The Manuscript Collection of about 60 manuscripts, including Deed from Indians to Edward Starbuck dated 1665, the oldest original Nantucket document known. Also William Worth's Book begun in 1662; Mary Starbuck letters 1714; Elihu Coleman's Tract Against Slavery 1729. (Fair St. Museum and see N.H.A. Proc. 1917, p. 33)

Collection Old Manuscripts Given by Mrs. Joseph B. Macy, containing Marriage Certificate of Peter Barnard and Anna Starbuck 1733; Deed from Seth Paddock to Eliphalet Paddock 1767; Will of William Worth 1777; Indenture Binding Son of Caleb Stratton and son of Ruth Clerk to Jonathan Paddock 1757; 3 Clearances From Port of Nantucket, etc. (Fair St. Museum)

Letter from Captain Perry Winslow to his wife (Files, Fair St. Museum)

2 Letters to Nathaniel Freeman 1796, 1 from Jonathan Jenkins and 1 from Selectmen (Rare Items, Vault, Fair St. Museum)

Original Papers of Obed Hussey Dealing with Patents and the Patents of the Harvester and Improvements (Vault, Fair St. Museum)

Framed Letter to Josiah Coffin, Esq. from the Nantucket Gaol in 1771, written by Thomas Arthur and signed, "The King's True and Faithful Prisoner, March 8, 1771" (Mrs. Lewis S. Edgarton, Nantucket)

Pollard Papers and Sanford Papers, genealogy (micro. Athen.)

Barney Papers, genealogy (Fair St. Museum)

Genealogy of Nantucket—*10 volumes of manuscript by Wm. C. Folger (Fair St. Museum)*

Approximately 110 manuscripts re Gardner & Starbuck deeds, land grants etc. as well as much miscellaneous Nantucket data (Yale Univ. Library, Hist. Manuscript Room, "Nantucket Papers", New Haven, Conn.)

"Echos from Nantucket's Oldest House"—*Anna Starbuck Jenks, 1904, (Crosby Coll.)*

Starbuck Account Book, "The First Whaling Merchant"—*(N.H.A. Proc. 1915)*

Pages of original diary and extracts made from diary of Kezia Coffin Fanning—*(Fair St. Museum). See N.H.A. Proc. 1939, and Hist. Nant. Oct., 1953 through Apr., 1959.*

MAPS AND CHARTS re NANTUCKET

1626 — America by Abraham Goos, Amsterdam (Fair St. Museum)
1630 — DeLaet, Joh. J., Nova Anglia Novum Belgium et Virginia (Library Congress Map Division)
1658 — Nova Anglia, by Johannes Jansonius (Fair St. Museum)
1675 — A Chart of the Coast of America by John Seeler (John Carter Brown Library, Providence, R.I.)
1676 — A Map of New England and New York by F. Lamb (Boston Public Library, Rare Book Room)
1678 — Plan Showing Original Layouts on Harbor—*Worth, N.H.A. Bull., Vol. 2, Bull. 1-7*
1682 — Niew England by Johannes van Kevlen, Amsterdam (Fair St. Museum)
1690 — Novi Belgie (etc.) by Nicolaum Visscher (Fair St. Museum)
1717 — Reproduction of the one known copy of a chart by Southack, printed at Boston, Mass., 1717 (Whaling Museum)

c. 1720 — Copy U.S.A. Geodetic Survey of Chart Found in the Public Record Office, London. Judged made by a British Naval Survey Party c. 1720. First real survey to show the islands (Whaling Museum)

1720 — Photostat copies of an elaborate map of the Coast from Navesink Highlands to Marblehead, made by an English Survey Party. (Vault, Fair St. Museum)

c. 1772 — Map of Island of Nantucket, from the book "Letters From an American Farmer", Crévecoeur, London, 1782. Map drawn for book by Dr. James Tupper, son of the Sheriff of Nantucket (Fair St. Museum and Athen.)

1776 — Nantucket Island by I.F.W. Des Barres, Esq. From Atlantic Neptune Atlas. Surveyed for English Government. Very rare early issue, without soundings (Whaling Museum)

1787 — Map in French Edition of "American Farmer's Letters", Crévecoeur, (Athen.)

1791 — Chart of Nantucket Shoals by Capt. Paul Pinkham. Published by John Norman, Newbury St., Boston. (The rarest of Nantucket maps, according to historian Everett U. Crosby) (Whaling Museum)

1798 — Chart from Hollands Surveys of the Coast of New England, in American Pilot (Map File, Fair St. Museum). Similar map in 1812 American Pilot, printed and sold by Andrew J. Allen, 66 State St., Boston.

1820 — Chart of Nantucket drawn by Thomas Mitchell, aged 11 (Fair St. Museum)

1830 — Map Made in Coffin School (Fair St. Museum)

1831 — Map of Nantucket Surveyed by J. Prescott, Lt. U.S. Army (Fair St. Museum)

1833 — Map of Town of Nantucket, by William Coffin Jr. Published by H. Clapp, Nantucket. This is the famous street map of unusual accuracy as to shape of houses and house lots, and with much data. (Original pen and ink at Fair St. Museum—Map at Registry of Deeds, Nantucket)

1838 — Map of the Island of Nantucket, including Tuckernuck, by William Mitchell, Lithographer E. W. Bouve, Boston. The first large size map and of considerable accuracy. (In Safe, Fair St. Museum)

1843 — Map of Nantucket by Peleg Coffin, Esq. and Others—"*American Biography*" *published by Harper & Bros. 1843*

1846 — Section of Town Destroyed by Fire, July 13, 1846 (Drawn by S. H. Jenks, Jr.) Bufford & Cos., Lith., Boston (On wall rear stairway Athen. and at Whaling Museum. Reproduced in "Ninety Five Per Cent Perfect", Crosby, 1953)

1846 — Nantucket Inquirer—*Issue of July 24, 1846. First page shows map of burnt district, cut from a leather carriage boot; the newspaper office had burned. (Fair St. Museum)*

1848 — Nantucket Harbor. U.S.A. Government Survey directed by A. D. Bache. The first accurate survey (Fair St. Museum)

1853 — Coast Survey, Maine to Nantucket (Map File, Fair St. Museum)

1854 — Chart of Nantucket Shoals (Fair St. Museum)

1856 — Map of Nantucket and Martha Vineyard, in "Papers Relating to the Island of Nantucket", Hough, 1856

1858 — Map of Counties of Barnstable, Dukes and Nantucket. Engraved by H. F. Wallings. Shows Nantucket in lower right, above which is street map of town and business directory. (Fair St. Museum & Whaling Museum)

1858 — Nantucket. Map of Streets of Town. With Owners' Names. Henry F. Wallings, Supt. of State (Reg. Deeds, Nantucket)

1860 — Chart of Coast, Monomoy, Nantucket Shoals to Block Island (Map File, Fair St. Museum)

1869 — Historical Map of Nantucket, by the Rev. F. C. Ewer, D.D. The Major & Knapp, Eng. Mfg. & Lith. Co., 71 Broadway, N.Y. The first issue had historical data through 1865. This is the largest, best-known and most useful Nantucket map, with important recording of old roads, Indian place-names and Proprietors' set-offs. (Entrance hall at Athen.) There were a number of printings, the first as above; a subsequent issue was by J. Ottmann, Lith., New York.

1881 — Birds' Eye View of the Town of Nantucket. Published by J. J. Stoner, Madison, Wis. (Whaling Museum and Fair St. Museum)

Roughly drawn maps of House Lot Section 1661-1663 and 1665-1680 (In Drawer of Case 4 (G) Fair St. Museum)

House Lot Map of Capaum Settlement 1665-1680 N.H.A. Bull. Vol. 2, Bull. 2 and 4

Remarks on Hubbard's Map of New England (1677) by Samuel Greene and Charles Deane, with fac-simile of original—*Proc. Mass. Hist. Soc., Nov. 1887 and 1888.*

"Cavo de Baros or The Place of Cape Cod in the Old Cartology"—*DeCosta, 1881 (Crosby Coll).*

Survey Plot, Property Containing Windmill. From Survey by Wm. F. Codd, Aug. 18, 1897 (Library Soc. Pres. N.E. Antiquities, Boston)

Map of Nantucket Showing Street Names, Railroad Line and Important Buildings—*J. H. Robinson, 1905 (Lib. Cong. Map Division)*

1912 Assessors' Map, Updated by George W. Jones 1963-1968 (Assessors' Office, Nantucket)

Map of Town of Nantucket with Streets Shown and Named—*J. H. Robinson, 1928*

Map of Town of Nantucket to Trotts Hills—*Wm. F. Swift, Surveyor, 1935*

Land Court Map of Island, Plotted in Numbered Squares; Cases to Jan. 1, 1931 (On Wall Assessors' Office, Nantucket)

General Highway Map of Nantucket County, Mass.—*Dept. Public Works 1939 (Lib. Cong.)*

Map Showing Changes Made in Streets After Fire of 1846 (Map Drawer, Registry Deeds, Nantucket)

"A Plat of the Roads in the Town Pasture Laid Out by the Agents of the Proprietors, Nantucket, 10 mo. 27th, 1821" (Proprietors' Book of Plans #1, p. 72, Registry Deeds, Nantucket)

Map of Historic District—*Hist. Nant., Apr. 1956*

Map of Historic Buildings—*Hist. Nant., July, 1957*

Main Street in Whaling Days—*Hist. Nant., Oct. 1957*

Maps in Attic 75 Main St., Nantucket—*Recording by Stackpole, 1959 (N.H.A.)*

The Name of Nantucket on Early Maps—*"Nantucket in Print", Crosby, 1946*

Other Maps and Plans (Map Drawer and Proprietors' Book of Plans. Registry Deeds, Nantucket)

Nantucket Zoning Map Prepared by Shurcliff & Merrill, Boston, 1968 (Office of Clerk of Courts, Nantucket)

MARIA MITCHELL

Maria Mitchell's Notes on Weather Sept. 1846 to Dec. 1849 (micro. Athen.)

Notes Taken While Librarian of Atheneum, 1850-1853-1854-1856 (micro. Athen.)

Correspondence re the King of Denmark's Comet Medal Awarded Miss M. Mitchell—*Everett, 1849 (Athen.)*

"Women of the Century"—*Hanaford, 1876*

"Maria Mitchell, Life, Letters & Journals"—*Kendall, 1896*

Women of Nantucket—*N.H.A. Proc. 1912, p. 31*

Eminent Nantucketers—*"Nantucket: a History", Douglas-Lithgow, 1914*

Maria Mitchell—*N.H.A. Proc. 1923*

"Recollections of Lydia S. Hinchman", 1929 (M. M. Library)

"Sweeper in the Sky"—*Wright, 1949*

"Two Steps Down"—*Shurrocks, 1953*

"The Lady Who Kept Looking"—*Wright and Bennett, 1958 (Pamphlet M. M. Assoc.)*

Maria Mitchell—*Hist. Nant., Oct. 1959 and Jan. 1967*

Fifty Famous Nantucketers—*Vol. 56, G.B.G. Scrapbooks (micro. Athen.)*

MARIA MITCHELL ASSOCIATION

See Organizations

Publications of Maria Mitchell Association

MARITIME

"The Maritime History of Massachusetts 1783-1860"—*Morrison, 1921*

MAYFLOWER DESCENDANTS IN NANTUCKET FAMILIES

Mayflower Descendants—*N.H.A. Proc. 1906, p. 32-43*

MELVILLE, HERMAN

"Moby Dick or The White Whale"—*Melville, 1851*
Melville—*"Nantucket in Print", Crosby, 1946*
Melville and Nantucket—*Heflin, N.H.A. Proc. 1951*

MEN AND WOMEN OF NANTUCKET

See Name of Each.
Heads of Families, Massachusetts First Census—*U.S. Census 1790 (Athen.)*
Individual Bound Volumes of Biographies by Dr. Wm. E. Gardner of the following: Frederick Coleman Sanford; Moses Joy Jr.; Charles A. Selden; Peter Folger; George Fawcett; Roy Hawkes Gilpatrick; William E. Gardner (micro. Athen.)
Fifty Famous Nantucketers—*Vol. 56, G.B.G. Scrapbooks (micro. Athen.)*
Who's Who in Nantucket; Biographies of 87 Nantucketers Prominent in 1942—*Vol. 60 G.B.G. Scrapbooks (micro. Athen.)*
Women of Nantucket—*N.H.A. Proc. 1912*
"Women of the Century"—*Hanaford, 1876*
Eminent Nantucketers—*"Nantucket; a History", Douglas-Lithgow, 1914*
"The Richest Men of Massachusetts"—*Forbes, 1852 (Athen.)*
"Rich Men of Massachusetts"—*Redding & Co., 1852 (Athen.)*
Distinguished Nantucketers—*Notebook of Annie Alden Folger, 1931 (micro. Athen.)*
Illustrious Sons and Daughters—*"Nantucket Odyssey", Guba, 1951*
"Nantucket Characters"—*Wyer, 1892*

MERIDIAN STONES

Stones Scraped and Re-Lettered—*N.H.A. Proc. 1896, p. 21*
Documentation of Meridian Stones for H.A.B.S. 1936 (Lib. Cong.)
Meridian Stones—*History of Pacific National Bank Building Done for H.A.B.S. (Athen.)*

MICROFILMED MATERIAL

At Atheneum
  60 Scrapbooks Compiled by Grace Brown Gardner on Nantucket Subjects
  Nantucket Newspapers to Date
  Logbooks and Journals as Listed Under Logbooks
  Many of the Older Nantucket Books, as Listed Under Books
At Town Building, Nantucket
  All Records to Date in Registry of Deeds
At Whaling Museum
  Logbooks and Journals as Listed Under Logbooks

MIGRATIONS

Migrations—*Vol. 6, G.B.G. Scrapbooks (micro. Athen.)*
Migrations from Nantucket to Hudson, N.Y.—*N.H.A. Proc. 1928*
Nantucketers' Migrations South and West—*N.H.A. Proc. 1933*
An Exile From Home—*N.H.A. Proc. 1946*
The Dunkirk Colony in 1797—*Proc. N.H.A. 1945*
The Nantucket Migrations—*Stackpole, Hist. Nant., Oct. 1958*
A Trip to Lahaina in Sandwich Islands—*Hist. Nant. Jan. 1968*

MILESTONES

Milestones Were Placed 100 Years Ago—*I. & M. June 14, 1924*

MILFORD HAVEN, WALES

"The Builders of Milford"—*Thomas, England, 1920 (Athen.)*
"Purely Local", Greville and the Quakers—*Thomas, Cardiff, 1935 (Athen.)*
Emigrations from Nantucket—*"Nantucket Odyssey", Guba, 1951*
"The Sea Hunters"—*Stackpole, 1953*
"The Story of Milford"—*Rees, 1954 (See Hist. Nant. Jan. 1957)*
Nantucketers Build a Whaling Town in Wales—*Jones, Hist. Nant. Apr. 1955*
Nantucket's Colony in the Old World—*Dell, Hist. Nant., July, 1955*
A Visit to Milford Haven—*Jones, Hist. Nant., Jan. 1957*

MILLS

Fulling Mill—*N.H.A. Proc. 1902, p. 20*
The Old Mill—*N.H.A. Proc. 1946 (also data re other mills)*
Mills—*"Glacier's Gift", Wilson, 1911*
Old Windmill—*"Nantucket; a History", Douglas-Lithgow, 1914*
The Round-Top Mill; Mill-Stone From This Now Base of Soldiers' & Sailors' Monument—*N.H.A. Proc. 1917*
The Old Mill, Its History and Tradition—*Turner, "100 Years on Nantucket", I. & M. 1921*
Round-Top Grist Mill—*"100 Years on Nantucket", I. & M. 1921*
Notes on Some Windmills in New England—*Wailes, Old Time New England, Boston, Jan. 1938*
Grist Mill at Lily Pond 1666—*"Early Nantucket and Its Whale Houses", Forman 1966, p. 25*
Old Mill—*Vol. 18 G.B.G. Scrapbooks (micro. Athen.)*
Views of Mills: Painting of Round-Top Mill, by James Walter Folger, 1908 (Fair St. Museum); *"The Port Folio"—Sansom, Vol. V, 1811, p. 32; "Barber's Historical Collections", 1839*

MINIATURES

Miniatures—*see Pictures*

MITCHELL, WILLIAM

William Mitchell—*N.H.A. Proc. 1949*
See Maria Mitchell

MODELS

Whale Models (Tap Room, Jared Coffin House)
See Ship Models

MONOMOY

Plans of Monomoy Heights—*Drawn by Wm. F. Codd, 1889 (Map Case, Registry Deeds, Nantucket)*

MONUMENT, SOLDIERS & SAILORS

Monument—*"The Island of Nantucket", Godfrey, 1882*
Monument—*"Argument Settlers", Turner, 1966, p. 48*
Mill-Stone From Round-Top Mill Used for Base—*N.H.A. Proc. 1917*
The Monument—*"Nantucket: a History", Douglas-Lithgow, 1914*

MOTHS

See Insects

MOTT, LUCRETIA

"Lucretia, the Quakeress"—*Hanaford, 1856*
Lucretia Mott—*Harper's Weekly, May 21, 1870*
"James and Lucretia Mott"—*Hallowell, 1884*
Women of Nantucket—*N.H.A. Proc. 1912*
Eminent Nantucketers—*"Nantucket: a History", Douglas-Lithgow, 1914*
Lucretia Mott—*"100 Years on Nantucket", I. & M. 1921*

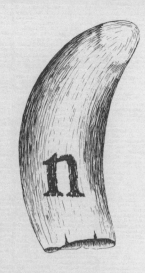

Illustrious Sons and Daughters—*"Nantucket Odyssey", Guba, 1951*
"Lucretia Mott, Girl of Old Nantucket"—*Burnett, 1951 (fiction)*
Lucretia Coffin Mott—*N.H.A. Proc. 1912 and Hist. Nant. Oct. 1967*

MUSEUM, FAIR STREET

Fair Street Museum, N.H.A.—*Publications and advertising pamphlets*

MUSKEGET

Muskeget, History of—*Worth, N.H.A. Bull., Vol. 2, Bull. 1*
Muskeget—*Vol. 31, G.B.G. Scrapbooks (micro. Athen.)*
Muskeget and Nantucket Quadrangles—*Mass. Geodetic Survey, 1929*
The Sands of Muskeget—*Phillips, n.d. (Athen.)*

MUTINIES

"The Globe Mutiny"—*Lay & Hussey, 1828*
"Life of Samuel Comstock, the Terrible Whaleman"—*Wm. Comstock, 1840*
Finding of Mutineers of Ship Bounty—*N.H.A. Proc., 1918, p. 15*
"Mutiny at Midnight"—*Stackpole, 1938*
The Globe Mutiny—*N.H.A. Proc. 1951*
Special Exhibit of Letters, Maps, Books and Manuscripts re Globe Mutiny
    (Library, Whaling Museum)

MC CLEAVE

Mrs. McCleave and Her Museum—*"Spun-Yarn From Old Nantucket", Wyer, 1914*
Framed Picture of Interior of McCleave Museum, Main Street, and Notice of
    Auction Sale Held There (In Storeroom, Fair St. Museum)
See Recordings

N

NANTUCKET COUNTY

Incorporated 1695—*N.H.A. Proc. 1920, p. 37*

NANTUCKET, THE NAME

"The Island of Nantucket", Godfrey, 1882
Amerind Place Names—*"Nantucket: a History", Douglas-Lithgow, 1914*
Early Names of Islands—*Worth, N.H.A. Bull., Vol. 2, Bull. 1*
"Nantucket in Print", Crosby, 1946
Nantucket Place Names—*"Nantucket Odyssey", Guba, 1951*

NATURAL HISTORY

"The Outer Lands"—*Sterling, 1967*
See Maria Mitchell Assoc. for Publications

NAVIGATION

Sunset Longitude—*N.H.A. Proc. 1928, p. 47*

NAVY ON NANTUCKET

Navy on Nantucket—*Hist. Nant., Jan. 1964*

NEIGHBORS, NANTUCKET

Nantucket Neighbors—*"Argument Settlers", Turner, 1966, p. 118*
Nantucket Neighbors—*(Records of Nantucket Civic League)*

NEWBEGIN FAMILY

Newbegin Family—*"Nantucket Centennial Celebration", Dudley, 1895, p. 16*
The Newbegins—*"The Island Fairie" (newspaper), Aug. 8, 1870*

NEWCOMEN SOCIETY

William Rotch—*Stackpole, Address to Newcomen Society Meeting, 1950*

NEWSPAPERS, NANTUCKET

Nantucket Newspapers—*(On file and on micro. at Athen.)*
Nantucket Newspapers—*(Bound Copies at Fair St. Museum)*
Inquirer & Mirror Newspapers—*(Files at I. & M.)*
Journalism in Nantucket—*"The Island of Nantucket", Godfrey, 1882*
History of Nantucket Newspapers—*Turner, "100 Years on Nantucket" I. & M. 1921*
Nantucket's Newspapers—*Starbuck, N.H.A. Proc. 1902, p. 11*
Nantucket Newspapers—*Hoadley, Hist. Nant., Oct. 1955*
The Newspapers of Nantucket—*"Nantucket: a History", Douglas-Lithgow, 1914*
Newspapers—*"Brief Historical Data", Farnum, 1915*
First Newspaper Published on Nantucket—*"Argument Settlers", Turner, 1966. p. 25*
A Century & a Half of Nantucket Newspapers—*Stackpole, I. & M., May 29, 1969*
Newspapers Published on Nantucket

Nantucket Gazette	1816
The Nantucket Weekly Magazine	1817
The Inquirer	1821
The Nantucket Journal	1826
The Islander	1840
The Weekly Telegraph	to 1845
The Mirror	1845
The Weekly Warder	1845
The Nantucket Weekly Mirror	c.1864
The Inquirer and Mirror	1865
The Island Fairie	1870
The Island Review	1874
The Nantucket Journal	1878
The Coffin School Record	1884
The 'Sconset Pump	1888
The 'Sconset Visiter	1889
The Cobbles	1919
The Nantucket Beacon	1930
The Madaket Free Press	1940
The Sea Chest (High School Publ.)	to 1940
The Islander (High School Publ.)	1940
The Nantucket Town Crier	1947
Moby Dick News	1947
The Wailer	July 2, 1961

The Harpoon	1934-1937
The Nantucket Light	1964

I. & M. Supplements and Other Extras

Inquirer Extra Containing Account of Burning of the Asylum	1844
Grand Masonic Festival; 100th Anniversary of Union Lodge of Nantucket, June 27,	1871
Relief Association Supplement	1880
Bicycle Supplement	1896
School Supplement	1889
Siasconset's Gala Week	1903
The Oldest House Supplement	1907
Ice Embargo Supplement	1912
Peace Extra	Nov. 11, 1918
100 Years on Nantucket	1921
Hospital Fete Supplement	1929
Nantucket Island Supplement	1933
Freeze-Up Supplement	1934
Fourth of July Parade Supplement	1939
50th Anniversary Old Press, on Gold Stock	1940
Special 'Sconset Edition	1947
Fire Supplement	1949
Storm Supplement	1952

NEW YORK

Transfer of Island from New York to Massachusetts—*N.H.A. Proc. 1930*

"Papers Relating to the Island of Nantucket While Under the Colony of New York"—*Hough, 1856*

The Secession and Annexation of Nantucket—*Cornish, The Green Bag, Mar. 1899*

NOVA SCOTIA

Nova Scotia—"*History of Nantucket*"—*Starbuck, 1924*

"Nantucket Odyssey", Guba, 1951

"The Sea Hunters", Stackpole, 1953

Benefit for Halifax Fire Sufferers—*Hist. Nant., Apr. 1957, p. 19*

OCEAN HOUSE (JARED COFFIN HOUSE of the NANTUCKET HISTORICAL TRUST)

History of Building done for H.A.B.S. (Lib. Cong. and Athen.)

Restoration and History—*Hist. Nant., Apr. 1962*

O'CONOR, CHARLES

Charles O'Conor—*Frank Leslie's Illustrated Newspaper, May 24, 1884*
Charles O'Conor—*Magazine of American History, June, 1885*
Portrait of Hon. Charles O'Conor (Fair St. Museum)

OLDEST HOUSE (JETHRO COFFIN HOUSE)

Oldest House—*see Publications of N.H.A.*
Blueprints Made for Use in Restoration (Fair St. Museum and Soc. Pres. N.E. Antiq.)
Purchase of House and Restoration—*N.H.A. Proc. 1924; 1925; 1926; 1927 and 1928*
History of Building done for H.A.B.S. (Lib. Cong. and Athen.)
"Echoes From Nantucket's Oldest House"—*Jenks, 1904*
"The Oldest House on Nantucket Island"—*Coffin, 1905*
The Oldest House—*I. & M. Supplement, Aug. 17, 1907*
Historic Oldest House—*"100 Years on Nantucket", I. & M. 1921*
"Nantucket's Oldest House"—*Macy, 1929*

ORGANIZATIONS AND CLUBS

Organizations and Clubs—*Vol. 24, G.B.G. Scrapbooks (micro. Athen.)*
Societies, Clubs and Institutions—*"Nantucket: a History", Douglas-Lithgow, 1914*
Clubs, etc.—*Hist. Nant., Apr. 1957, p. 15-16*
Agricultural Society—*Hist. Nant., Apr. 1957; Vol. 30, G.B.G. Scrapbooks (micro. Athen.); Records of Nantucket Agricultural Society 1856-1891 (Athen.)*
Admiralty Club—*Recording made in 1959 (N.H.A.)*
Civic League—*Nantucket Neighbors—"Argument Settlers", Turner, 1966, p. 118*
Records of Nantucket Debating Society from 1836 to 1842 (Fair St. Museum)
Maria Mitchell Association—*Pamphlets of the Assoc.*
Free Masonry—*Starbuck, N.H.A. Bull., Vol. III, Bull. 1, 1903*
"History of Union Lodge, F. & A. M., 1771-1941"—*Turner, 1941*
Union Lodge of Nantucket—*N.E. Freemason, Sept., 1874*
Grand Masonic Festival; 100th Anniversary of Union Lodge, Nantucket—*I. & M. Extra June 27, 1871*
Ladies' Howard Society—*N.H.A. Proc. 1919, p. 16*
Momus Club—*Hist. Nant., Apr. 1957*
Monnohanit Club—*New Bedford Standard Times, 1926*
Nantucket Social Reading Society—*N.H.A. Proc. 1925*
Pacific Club—*"Nantucket: a History", Douglas-Lithgow, 1914*
Pacific Club—*History of Building Done for H.A.B.S. (Athen.)*
Relief Association—*I. & M. Supplement, Jan. 24, 1880*
The Sherburne Lyceum—*N.H.A. Proc. 1923, p. 53*
Sorosis Women's Club—*Hist. Nant., June, 1964, p. 20*
Yacht Club—*Recording Made in 1959 (N.H.A.)*
Wharf Rat Club—*Recording by Davis, 1959 (N.H.A.)*
Wharf Rat Club—*New Bedford Standard Times, July, 1953*
  The following are mentioned in "Island of Nantucket", Godfrey, 1882: Fragment Society; Children's Aid Society; Odd Fellows; Daughters of Rebekah; Union Benevolent Society; Women's Christian Temperance Union

ORGANS

See Churches

OUT OF TOWN

See Place Name of Each Location

P

PAINTERS

Painters Who Have Worked at Nantucket in the Past—*Coffin, 1968 (Athen.)*

PAINTINGS

See Artists

See Pictures

See Portraits

Some Important Paintings are as follows:

"Town of Sherburne, Nantucket Island", earliest known painting of Nantucket— by Thomas Birch, after 1806. See records of Atheneum Trustees' Meeting Oct., 1960; also see "Antiques", Apr. 1966. (Main Room, Athen.)

"Cranberry Bog"—Rae Carpenter (Librarian's Room, Athen.)

Ship "Samuel Russell, built 1840" (North Wall, Athen.)

Ship "Surprise", built 1857 (North Wall, Athen.)

Paintings brought from China for Frederick C. Sanford: 4 ships and 5 Chinese paintings of scenes in Houqua's Gardens, Canton, c. 1840. See Trustees of Atheneum Records 1892-1945, p. 40. Also I. & M. 1956. (Great Hall, 2nd floor, Athen.)

"Main Street Before the Fire"—attributed to Hathaway (West Wall Main Floor, Athen.)

"Ship Spermo of Nantucket" (Rear Stairway Athen.)

"Father's Gone A-Whaling"—Mural by Sheila Barney Jelleme (North Wall Children's Room, Athen.)

2 Views of Interior Old Mill—Wendell Macy (Starr Lawrence Kynett Memorial Room, Athen.)

"Sketch of Nantucket"—Carleton Wiggins (Starr Lawrence Kynett Memorial Room, Athen.)

Primitive of "S.S. Sacramento" (Whaling Museum)

"Whaling in the Arctic" (Whaling Museum)

2 small paintings, by J. Walter Folger (Whaling Museum)

Rare Old Paintings of Whaling Scenes (Walls of Stairway and Second Floor Corridor, Whaling Museum)

Ship Levi Starbuck (Fair St. Museum)

Steamer "Telegraph", James Walter Folger (Fair St. Museum)

Steamer "Island Home", Wendell Macy (Fair St. Museum)

Nantucket Harbor from Monomoy, Col. Julian Yates (Vestibule Wall, Fair St. Museum)

Nantucket Auction, Col. Julian Yates (2nd floor Fair St. Museum)

Representative Group of Paintings Given by Nantucket Artists to Nantucket Foundation Inc. as a Permanent Collection. (Listed, Stored and Exhibited at Kenneth Taylor Galleries, Nantucket)

Collection of Paintings by Ruth Haviland Sutton, (Jared Coffin House, Nantucket)

Nantucket Scene 1893—Wendell Macy (Macy Bldg., Hist. Trust, Nantucket)

PARK AND RECREATION COMMISSION

Recreation and Parks, Nantucket, Mass.—Prepared for Commission by National Recreation Assoc., N.Y., Aug., 1961 (W. Ripley Nelson, owner)

PATENT, DONGAN
Deed (In Wall Case Registry Deeds, Nantucket)

PATTERSON
Capt. David G. Patterson's Documents, Chronometer Box and Sextant
(Whaling Museum)

PEASE FAMILY
Pease Family—*I. & M. July 19, 1873*

PEIRCE, CYRUS
Cyrus Peirce—*N.H.A.Proc. 1909, p. 41*
Journals of Cyrus Peirce and Mary Swift, 1928 (Athen.)
Picture of Cyrus Peirce (Fair St. Museum) with Biography in Museum Files.
See Schools

PHOTOGRAPHS
Turner Collection of c. 400 glass plates of old Nantucket from 1845 to 1912 (In
6 Boxes in Vestibule Closet, Fair St. Museum)
6 Loose-Leaf Albums of Pictures Made from the Above Plates (Fair St.
Museum)
Exhibition of Old Slides—*Nelson, Hist. Nant., Oct. 1963*
Henry S. Wyer and Henry Platt Collections Slides (Fair St. Museum)
Stereoptican Pictures Nantucket Streets and Houses (Fair St. Museum and
1800 House)
c. 131 Stereo Views of Nantucket: People, Houses, Ships, Scenes of Last Quarter
19th Century (Soc. Pres. N.E. Antiq.)
Alexander Starbuck Collection 10 Bound Albums Postcards: 600 Old Views
of Nantucket (2nd floor Closet Fair St. Museum)
Postcard Collection: c. 900 Views Nantucket (Soc. Pres. N.E. Antiq.)
Photos Old Nantucket Houses (Library Soc. Pres. N.E. Antiq. and Fair St.
Museum)
I. & M. Calendar Nantucket Photographs from 1914 (Athen.)
"Aerial Views of Nantucket"—*Lang, 1926*
"Fifty Glimpses of Nantucket Island from Photos"—*Murphy, 1897*
"Nantucket, Old & New, Centennial Edition"—*Wyer, 1895*
"106 Views of Nantucket"—*J. J. Robinson, 1911*
10 Views of Nantucket Wharves (Charles F. Sayle, Nantucket)
Photos of Shearing Scenes (Wall, 2nd floor Fair St. Museum)
Photo Wharf at New Bedford Showing Ship Niger (Fair St. Museum)
Ship Hero (Fair St. Museum)
Ship Pacific (Fair St. Museum)
See Steamers for Photographs of Steamers
Nantucket From Brant Point 1895—*H. S. Wyer (Shows panorama of Harbor,
etc.) (Fair St. Museum)*
Panorama of Brant Point Section c. 1880, Before Buildings (Owner: David W.
Austin, Nantucket)
1965 Aerial Photograph for Mass. Dept. Public Works (Sherburne Associates,
O Main St., Nantucket)
Collections of Daguerreotypes and Miniatures (Case 22, 2nd floor, Fair St.
Museum)
Collection of Silhouettes, including those of David Mitchell, William Mitchell,
Ruth Gardner, Eben Coleman, Judith Hussey, Mary Ann Hussey, Albert
Gardner, Lydia B. Hussey, E. M. Bartlett, Capt. Joseph Chase Jr., Elihu
Coleman and wife, Walter Folger and wife (Show Case #1, 2nd Floor, Fair
St. Museum)
Many Photographs of Nantucket People, including:
Eben W. Allen
Capt. Edward C. Austin

Jacob Barker
Mrs. Eliza Barney
Mrs. Mary Barnard
Cromwell Barnard
Sarah Barnard
Benjamin F. Brown
Moses Brown
Mrs. Charlotte Chase Coffin
Moses Ellis
Walter Emerson
Ferdinand C. Ewer
Alexander Mirabeau Folger
Judge Charles J. Folger
George Howland Folger
Robert F. Gardner
Dorcas Honorable
Hosier Family
Mary Hussey-Earle
Alfred Macy
Lucretia Mott
Maria Mitchell
Eliza Ann McCleave
Capt. Joseph Mitchell
Eliza W. Mitchell
Wm. Mitchell and dau. Maria
Eunice Paddock
Cyrus Peirce
Mr. and Mrs. F. C. Sanford
Charles H. Starbuck
George Winslow
(Fair St. Museum)

PICTURES AND PRINTS

Print "Town of Sherburne", Engraved by B. Tanner, Portfolio No. 5, p. 30, Phila. 1811. See N.H.A. Proc. 1948

Allan Forbes Collection Whaling Pictures—*Hist. Nant. Apr. 1961*

Print, "Mexican News", by Alfred Jones after A. C. Woodville (Librarian's Room, Athen.)

"Franklin at the Court of France in 1788"—*Hand Colored Engraving of Painting by Baron Jolly (East Parlor 1800 House)*

5 Pictures of the Abandonment of the Whalers in the Arctic Ocean in 1871 (Fair St. Museum)

Picture of Fire of 1836 (Fair St. Museum)

Ship Lady Adams, built 1801, James Colesworthy, Master (Fair St. Museum)

Ship Walter Scott (Fair St. Museum)

"Death of Washington" (Fair St. Museum)

Sperm Whaling: "The Chase" and "The Capture", pair Old Prints 1853 (Whaling Museum)

5 Colored Wood Carved Nantucket Pictures—*J. Walter Folger (Fair St. Museum)*

2 Lithographs of Boston Tea Party, 1 by Sarony & Major and 1 by N. Currier (Whaling Museum)

Collection Etchings of Whaling Scenes by George Gale (Whaling Museum)

Various Pictures of Whaleships & Whaling (Scrimshaw Rm. Whaling Museum)

Rare Old Whaling Lithographic Prints (Walls of Stairway and 2nd Floor Corridor Whaling Museum)

Ink Drawings of "Fleet Ready for Sea" and "View of Boston Harbor"—*George Marshall (Whaling Museum)*

About 75 Pictures of Nantucket Scenes or by Nantucket Artists, in Permanent Collection of Nantucket Foundation, Inc. (Stored, Listed and Exhibited at Kenneth Taylor Galleries, Nantucket)

Chromo-Lithograph Collection of E. U. Crosby (Owned by Nantucket Foundation Inc. and Stored and Exhibited at Kenneth Taylor Galleries, Nantucket. List on File. See "Chromos", Crosby, 1954)

View of Nantucket, c. 1820—*W. Barber. Engraved by S. E. Brown, Boston (Fair St. Museum)*

Main & Federal Streets, Listing Businesses & Owners—*Drawing by Wm. H. Gardner, c. 1834 (Fair St. Museum)*

Nantucket Town from Monomoy 1884—*Lithograph by Wendell Macy (Whaling Museum and Jared Coffin House of Nantucket Historical Trust)*

"Nantucket Woodcuts"—*Naoko Matsubara, with Text by Fritz Eichenberg, 1967*

See Photographs

See Portraits

PINKHAM FAMILY

Lieut. Alexander B. Pinkham—*N.H.A. Proc. 1943, p. 16*

Portrait of Lieut. Alexander B. Pinkham (Fair St. Museum)

Capt. Seth Pinkham—*"Through the Hawse Hole", Anderson, 1932*

PITCAIRN ISLAND

Log of Ship Topaz, Mentioning Discovery of Rendezvous of Perpetrators of Bounty Mutiny, dated 1808 (Whaling Museum)

Finding of Mutineers of Ship Bounty—*N.H.A. Proc. 1918, p. 15*

"The Story of Yankee Whaling"—*Shapiro & Stackpole, 1959*

"Nantucket Odyssey"—*Guba, 1951*

PLAGUE

Plague—*"Argument Settlers", Turner, 1966, p. 15*

See Indians

PLANE CRASHES

Northeast Airlines Plane Crash—*Nantucket Town Crier, Aug. 22, 1958 and I. and M. August, 1958*

Radar Plane Crash—*Boston Herald, Apr. 26, 1967*

POCOMO

Pocomo through Wauwinet—*Vol. 32, G.B.G. Scrapbooks (micro. Athen.)*

Pocomo—*"The Island of Nantucket", Godfrey, 1882, p. 243*

Pocomo Farm—*Proprietors' Book of Plans #1, p. 82 (Registry Deeds, Nantucket)*

POETRY, EARLY

Poets and Poetry—*"The Island of Nantucket", Godfrey, 1882, p. 244*

POLLARD PAPERS

Genealogy, as prepared by Miss Eliza Pollard (micro. Athen.)

POLPIS

A Boy on a Polpis Farm—*"Brief Historical Data", Farnham, 1915*

Early Tide Mills at Polpis—*"The Glacier's Gift", Wilson, 1911*

Old Polpis—*Chadwick, N.H.A. Proc. 1922 and Hist. Nant. Jan. 1958*

"Nantucket Odyssey", Guba, 1951

"Polpis Past and Present"—*Marshall, 1962*

Polpis—*Forman, Hist. Nant. Jan. 1962*

PONDS

Ponds of Nantucket—*Vol. 31, G.B.G. Scrapbooks (micro. Athen.)*

"Report of Committee on the Long Pond and Madaket Ditch, Town Meeting, March 20, 1882." Reprint I. & M., 1913 & 1954 (pamphlets)

Opinion Rendered Town of Nantucket by Henry B. Worth, Feb. 1911 re Rights of the Public in the Great Ponds—*I. & M. Feb. 1911*

"Law of the Seashore, Tidewaters and Great Ponds in Massachusetts and
  Maine"—*Whittesey, 1932 (Athen.)*
Ponds—*"The Island of Nantucket", Godfrey, 1882*
Ponds—*"Nantucket: a History", Douglas-Lithgow, 1914*
Fisheries of the Great Ponds—*Hist. Nant. Apr. 1965*
Fishing in Ponds—*"Argument Settlers", Turner, 1966, p. 157*
The Lily Pond—*Hist. Nant., Apr. 1968*

POOR FARM

Almshouse and Paupers—*"The Island of Nantucket", Godfrey, 1882, p. 12*
Inquirer Extra, Containing Account of Burning of the Asylum—*1844 (Fair St.
  Museum)*
See Quaise

PORTRAITS

Early Nantucket Artists—*Stark, Hist. Nant., July, 1958; Oct. 1958; Apr. 1959*
Painters Who Have Worked at Nantucket in the Past—*Coffin, 1968 (Athen.)*
Portraits of Nantucket Whaling Captains and Their Wives—*(Captains' Room,
  Whaling Museum) (List on File Whaling Museum)*
Over 100 Large Portraits—*(Walls of Fair St. Museum) (List on File)*
Portraits by William Swain, c. 1770-1847: Hon. Walter Folger Jr., Mrs. Timothy
  Clapp, Lieut. A. B. Pinkham, Arthur and Elizabeth Jones, Benjamin Gardner,
  Love Parker (Fair St. Museum) Mrs. William Plaskett, William Plaskett,
  Capt. Charles B. Swain, Mrs. Mary Chase (Whaling Museum)
  Charles G. Coffin—*(Great Hall, Athen.)*
  David Joy—*Reading Room, Athen.)*
  Benjamin Tucker and wife Mary Swain Tucker—*(Front Parlor, Hadwen
    House—Satler Memorial, Nantucket)*
  Capt. John Gardner and wife Eliza Worth Gardner—*(Mrs. Edward O.
    Gardner, Nantucket)*
Portraits by J. S. Hathaway, c. 1842: Large canvas of three children: William
  Coffin, Jared Coffin and Marianne Coffin—*(dining room, Jared Coffin House,
  Nantucket)*
  Augustus Morse, Edward R. Folger and wife Marianne, John Folger, Gideon
    Folger, Hon. Walter Folger Jr.—*(Fair St. Museum)*
  Rev. George Bradburn, Mrs. Judith Burnell—*(1800 House, N.H.A.)*
  Henry Coffin, Levi Starbuck, Charles Frederick Coffin, Susan Starbuck
    Coffin—*75 Main St., Nantucket)*
  Eunice Coffin, Levi Coffin—*(69 Main St., Nantucket)*
Portraits by George Fish, c. 1825-1906: William Hadwen and Mrs. Eunice
  Hadwen—*(dining room and back parlor, Hadwen House—Satler Memorial,
  N.H.A.)*
  Five Children of Matthew Starbuck, Priscilla Coleman Wyer, Katharine
    Starbuck and infant son Horace—*("Middle Brick", Main St., Nantucket)*
  Walter Folger, in Quaker attire; copy of Copley's portrait of Timothy Folger—
    (Athen.)
  2 large pastel paintings of young women—*(Jared Coffin House, Nantucket)*
  Pastel painting "The Seasons"—*(West Parlor, 1800 Ho. N.H.A.)*
Joseph Starbuck, painted by J. Bisbee—*("Middle Brick", Main St., Nantucket)*
Portraits by Elizabeth Rebecca Coffin—*(Coffin School, Nantucket, and
  Nantucket Cottage Hospital)*
Elizabeth Rebecca Coffin, painted by Thomas Eakins—*(Sewing Room. Coffin
  School, Nantucket)*
Admiral Sir Isaac Coffin—*(Paddock Room, Coffin School, Nantucket)*
Captain Charles Myrick, Robert Ratliff, Peter Folger—*painted by Eastman
  Johnson (Whaling Museum)*
Hon. Charles O'Conor, by Eastman Johnson—*(Fair St. Museum)*
Frederick Coleman Sanford, by Eastman Johnson—*(Athen.)*
Portraits of John B. Coffin, Joshua Coffin, and Captain Henry F. Coffin—
  (Mrs. Lewis S. Edgarton, Nantucket)
Portraits of James Cary (Captain) and of his Chinese Mandarin friend, Chung

Qua—*(Mrs. Allen R. Congdon, Nantucket)*
Dr. William E. Gardner, painted by Elmer Greene—*(Athen.)*
Abraham Quary, by Mrs. Hermione Dassel—*(Main Room, Athen.)*
Maria Mitchell, by Billings—*(Wall of Rear Stairway, Athen.)*
Col. Joseph C. Hart, photographic portrait—*(Great Hall, Athen.)*
Robert Barclay Fanning and wife Phoebe Swain Fanning—*(West bedroom, Hadwen House—Satler Memorial, N.H.A.)*
Captain Sanford Wilbur—*(Miss Dorothy Gardner, Siasconset, Mass.)*
Portraits of Judge Thaddeus C. Defriez, Judge Henry Riddell, and Judge George M. Poland—*(Registry of Probate, Nantucket)*
Portrait of Kezia Coffin Fanning—*(Mr. Frank B. Howard, Poughkeepsie, N. Y.)* Reproduced *N.H.A. Proc. 1939, p. 21.*
Portrait of Kezia Coffin Fanning in oils on tin—*(Mr. T. F. Wood III, New York City)*

POST-OFFICE

Nantucket Post-Office and the Post Masters—*"100 Years on Nantucket", I. & M. 1921*
The Siasconset Post-Office—*"100 Years on Nantucket", I. & M. 1921*

PRAIRIE DOGS

Prairie Dogs at Nantucket—*"Argument Settlers", Turner, 1966, p. 69*

PRESIDENTS

"When Presidents Visited the Island"—*"100 Years on Nantucket", I. & M., 1921*

PROBATES

Records of Probates and Wills—*(Files Probate Court, Nantucket County)*
Wills and Estates—*Worth, N.H.A. Bull., Vol. 2, Bull. 6 & 7*
Among the Probate Records—*N.H.A. Proc. 1914, p. 29-54*

PROPRIETORS

See Land

PUMP, 'SCONSET

'Sconset Pump—*N.H.A. Proc. 1923, p. 13 and 1925, p. 31*
Pump Square—*"Early Nantucket and Its Whale Houses", Forman, 1966*

Q

QUAISE

Story of Quaise Poor Farm—*J. Prescott, 1931 (Athen.)*
William B. Starbuck's Diary, Quaise, 1870-1873 (micro. Athen.)
Quaise—*"The Island of Nantucket", Godfrey, 1882, p. 266*
Quaise—*"Nantucket: a History", Douglas-Lithgow, 1914*
Poor Farm at Quaise—*"Nantucket Odyssey", Guba, 1951*
Quaise Poor Farm—*"Polpis Past and Present", Marshall, 1962*

QUAKERS AND QUAKERISM

Approx. 40 Volumes Friends' Books—*Nantucket Monthly Meeting Records (Vault, Fair St. Museum)*
Quakers—*Vol. 35 and 36, G.B.G. Scrapbooks (micro. Athen.)*
Quakers—*Outline of History Course for High School, Gardner (micro. Athen.)*
Copy of Map Showing Friends' Meetings in New England 1782 (In frame on wall Fair St. Meeting House)
12 Quaker Wedding Certificates (Framed on wall Meeting House)
Quaker Wedding Certificate, Clother Peirce and Lydia Hussey (Fair St. Museum)

Quaker Wedding Certificate, Susanna Paddock and Matthew Gardner. Among
    signers was Elihu Coleman (Mrs. Lewis S. Edgarton, Nantucket)
"The Works of Thomas Chalkley"—*Chalkley, 1791*
Quakerism on Nantucket Since 1800—*Worth, N.H.A. Bull., Vol. 1, Bull. 1, 1896*
Copy From Records of Friends' Meeting—*N.H.A. Proc. 1899*
The Dominion of the Quakers—*"Quaint Nantucket", Bliss, 1896*
The Original Quaker Hearse—*N.H.A. Proc. 1919*
Quakers, Decline of—*N.H.A. Proc. Vol. 1, Bull. 1, p. 3*
Nantucket and Its Quakers—*Prof. Cadbury, N.H.A. Proc. 1946*
An Off-Islander's Impressions—*Prof. Cadbury, N.H.A. Proc. 1949*
John Woolman in Nantucket—*N.H.A. Proc. 1940*
Two Quaker Teachers, John Boadle and Hepsibeth Hussey—*N.H.A. Proc. 1922*
The Frst Two Quaker Meeting-Houses on Nantucket—*N.H.A. Proc. 1950*
The Friends of Nantucket—*Winslow, N.H.A. Proc. 1936*
Quakers and Whalers in Nantucket—*Friends Intelligencer, 9th 24, 1949,*
    Phila., Pa.
Friends Meeting House—*Hist. Nant., July, 1954*
Quakerism on Nantucket—*Dell, N.H.A. Publication 1955*
Quaker Meeting Records—*Hist. Nant., Oct. 1958*
Friends Meeting—*Hist. Nant., July, 1964*
Quakerism in Nantucket—*Hist. Nant., July, 1965*
"Quakers and Slavery in America"—*Drake, 1950*
Quaker Meeting House—*"100 Years on Nantucket", I. & M. 1921*
Quakerism in Nantucket—*"Nantucket: a History", Douglas-Lithgow*
Friends Burial Ground—*"Nantucket Odyssey", Guba, 1951*
"Greville and the Quakers"—*"Purely Local", Thomas, 1935*
Quaker Preachers—*"Nantucket in Print", Crosby, 1946*
Nantucket Friends' Meeting, Summer 1967—*Seeler, Hist. Nant. July, 1968*

QUANNATA BANK

Quannata Bank 1808—*Proprietors Book of Plans #1, p. 56 (Registry Deeds,*
    Nantucket)

QUARTERBOARDS

Quarterboards—*Vol. 13, G.B.G. Scrapbooks (micro. Athen.)*
Ships' Quarterboards on Nantucket—*Stackpole, I. & M. June 26, 1937*
"Quarterboards on Nantucket"—*Stackpole, 1968 (booklet)*

QUARY, ABRAM

Abram Quary 1772-1850—*New Bedford Standard Times, Sept. 1, 1951*
Painting of Abram Quary by Mrs. Hermione Dassel, 1852 (Main floor west wall
    Athen.)
Record of Painting by Mrs. Dassel (Athen. Library Proprietors' Records,
    Vol. 1, p. 79)

Abraham Quary—*wood bas relief of Dassel painting, Aletha Macy, Carver (South Wall, Athen.)*
Daguerreotype of Quary (Athen.)
Legal Paper Signed by Abram Pinkham Quary Requesting Capt. Zenas Coffin to Pay Him for Services on Ship Lydia (Athen.)

QUIDNET

Quidnet—*"Nantucket Odyssey", Guba, 1951*
Quidnet—*"Island of Nantucket", Godfrey, 1882, p. 267*
The Hermit of Quidnet—*"Early Nantucket & Its Whale Houses"—Forman, 1966*

QUINCY, JOSIAH

Visit to Nantucket—*Proc. Mass. Hist. Soc., 2nd Series, Col. IV, 1887*

R

RAILROAD, NANTUCKET

Extensive Collection Railroad Memorabilia (Mrs. David Gray, Polpis, Nantucket)
Railroad—*Vol. 7 & 41 G.B.G. Scrapbooks (micro. Athen.)*
"The Nantucket Railroad 1880-1917"—*Island Service Co., Nantucket, Town Crier Press, Nantucket, 1947*
Nantucket Owned a Railroad—*Turner, "100 Years on Nantucket", I. & M. 1921*
Nine Miles of Railroad—*Beer, Yankee Magazine, July, 1956*
Railroads in Nantucket—*Hist. Nant., July, 1957*
Nantucket Railroad Stories—*Recording 1959 (N.H.A.)*
Survey for Railroad—*"Argument Settlers", Turner, 1966, p. 49*
Birth and Death of Nantucket Railroad—*Hist. Nant., Jan. 1963*
Nantucket's Railroads—*Hist. Nant. July, 1966*
Action and Dionis—*Ackerman, Yankee Magazine, July, 1968*
Nantucket's Railroad, 1881-1917—*I. & M. Calendar Photos 1969*

RATLIFF, ROBERT

Robert Ratliff—*"Nantucket, the Far-Away Island", Stevens, 1936*
Portrait of Ratliff by Eastman Johnson (On Wall in Lobby, Whaling Museum)

RECIPES

See Cook-Books

RECORDINGS

Recordings on Nantucket Subjects—*Hist. Nant., Apr. 1963*
33 Tape Recordings on Nantucket Subjects Made by Henry Coffin Carlisle in 1959, as follows (N.H.A. Owned)
1. Whaling—*Will Tripp*
2. Talk as Given at Whaling Museum—*Cartwright*
3. Old South Church Bell—*Gibbs*
4. Haulover Opening—*Mackay*
5. Coffin School—*Appleton and Gurley*
6. 75 Main Street Attic—*Gardner*
7. Old Nantucket—*Robinson and Pease*
8. Wharf Rat Club—*Davis*
9. Humor in Nantucket—*Gardner*
10. Admiralty Club—*skit*
11. Early Tuckernuck—*Gurley*
12. Maps in 75 Main St. Attic—*Stackpole*
13. Sinking of the Wanderer—*Tripp*
14. Brick Houses—*Gardner*
15. Yacht Club—*Davis and Gifford*

16. Jetties Clam Bed—*King*
17. Sconset Actor Colony—*Wilson*
18. Madaket—*Ray and Runk*
19. Sinking of Nantucket Lightship—*Tripp*
20. Fish, Shellfish and Lobsters—*McCleave and King*
21. Stone Fleet—*Tripp*
22. Tuckernuck—*Ramsdell*
23. Old North Wharf—*Walling*
24. Scrap Books—*Gardner*
25. Sconset and the Actor Colony—*Everett*
26. Lightship Baskets—*Reyes*
27. Ivory Whale Carving—*Macy*
28. Weather Bureau—*Grimes*
29. Nantucket Familiar Sounds
30. Nantucket Central Railroad Stories
31. Ice-boating at 92—*Ditmars*
32. Nantucket Central Railroad
33. Gibbs Pond Cranberry Bog

RECORDS

See Town Offices by Name.

5 Volumes "Vital Records of Nantucket, Mass. to the Year 1850"—*New England Historic Genealogical Society, Boston, 1928 (Athen.)*

List of Private Records of Vital Statistics, p. 5 through 10, "Vital Records of Nantucket, Mass." (as above)

Missing Court Records—*N.H.A. Proc. 1901, p. 9-10*

Among the Probate Records—*N.H.A. Proc. 1914, p. 29-54*

Nantucket Records—*"Nantucket: a History", Douglas-Lithgow, 1914*

A Portion of the Records of the Nantucket Customs House, Discontinued in 1913 (Library, Whaling Museum)

Oldest Records: (Books 1 and 2 Registry Deeds, Nantucket) Also the Starbuck Account Book of 300 pages, which has the following on inside of cover, "Mary Starbuck Account Book with the Indians, begun in 1662. Nathaniel Jr. continued it." (Rare Items, Vault, Fair St. Museum)

REGISTRY OF DEEDS

Located at Registry of Deeds, Nantucket, are the following:

County Records of Deeds from 1659 to date, with indexes and maps

Records of Land Court

Dongan Patent (on east wall)

1858 Map of Streets of Town, Wallings (on south wall)

RELIGION

See Churches

See Quakers
Beginnings of Organized Religion—*"Nantucket Odyssey", Guba, 1951*

REMINISCENCES

Reminiscences—*Vol. 37 and 38 G.B.G. Scrapbooks (micro. Athen.)*
Reminiscences—*"September Days on Nantucket", Bliss, 1902*
Personal Reminiscences of Mrs. Eliza W. Mitchell, 1894-5 (Diary Box in Vault, Fair St. Museum)

REPRESENTATIVES

Nantucket's Representatives in National and State Legislatures—*N.H.A. Proc. 1911, p. 29*
List of Nantucket's Legislators Since 1780—*"100 Years on Nantucket", I. & M. 1921*

RESORT

Annual Publicity Booklets—*(Nantucket Island Chamber Commerce)*
Resort—*"Nantucket as a Health Resort"—Douglas-Lithgow, 1912*

RESOURCES

"Selected Resources of the Island of Nantucket"—*Publication #4 Cooperative Extension Service, Univ. of Mass. and U.S. Dept. Agriculture, 1967*

REVOLUTION

See Wars

ROPEWALKS

Nantucket Industries—*Jones, Hist. Nant., Jan. 1966, p. 8*
Ropewalks—*"History of Nantucket", Obed Macy, 1835, p. 17*
Industries—*Hist. Nant., Apr. 1957*

ROTCH, WILLIAM

William Rotch—*Stackpole, 1950 (Address to Newcomen Society)*
William Rotch—*N.H.A. Proc. 1930, p. 26*
"William Rotch of Nantucket"—*Jones, The American Friend Publishing Co., Phila. 1901*

S

SAMPLERS, ETC.

"The Fishing Woman on Boston Common", framed needlework done by Susanna Colesworthy 1765. Exhibited in 1941 at Museum of Fine Arts, Boston (1800 House)
Silk Tapestry Mourning Piece, made by Sally Folger, 1807 (1800 House)
Various Samplers, Shellwork and Mourning Pictures etc. (1800 House and Fair St. Museum)

SANFORD, FREDERICK COLEMAN

Scrapbook of F. C. Sanford, 1875 (micro. Athen.)
Scrapbook of F. C. Sanford, 1882 (micro. Athen.)
Dr. Will Gardner's Notes on Sanford Scrapbook (micro. Athen.)
Account Book of F. C. Sanford, 1823
Account Book of Outfits and Charges Against Crew of Ship Memnon, James E. Houghton, Master, 1852, Edward Field & F. C. Sanford, Agents (micro. Athen.)
List of Ships That Sailed From Nantucket Since 1815, With Remarks Connected With the Voyage. F. C. Sanford (micro. Athen.) End of Volume Also Contains List of Ships That Belonged to Nantucket Prior to 1800 and Names of Their Owners (micro. Athen.)

F. C. Sanford's Accounts (micro. Athen.)
Notes and Statistics of Whaling Long Ago by F. C. Sanford (micro. Athen.)
Sanford Biography by Dr. William E. Gardner (micro. Athen.)
Sanford Papers, as Prepared by Mr. Sanford's sister (micro. Athen.)
Frederick C. Sanford—*N. Y. Evening Post, 1887*
Frederick C. Sanford—*Stackpole, I. & M., Feb. 1960*

SATLER MEMORIAL

See Hadwen House—*Satler Memorial*

SAYINGS AND CUSTOMS

Will Gardner's Talk Before Historical Association on Humor in Nantucket.
Recording 1959 (N.H.A.)
"Old Sailors' Yarns"—*Capt. R. F. Coffin, 1884 (fiction) (Athen.)*
"Talks About Old Nantucket"—*Hussey, 1901*
The Humor of Nantucket—*N.H.A. Proc. 1904, p. 24*
Old Nantucket Sayings—*N.H.A. Proc. 1931, p. 27*
More Old Nantucket Sayings—*N.H.A. Proc. 1935, p. 27*
Old Nantucket Idioms and Customs—*"Nantucket, the Far-Away Island",*
Stevens, 1936
"Nantucket Scraps"—*Austin, 1883*
"Historical Data and Memories"—*Farnham, 1915*
"Nantucket Scrap Basket"—*Macy, 1916*
"Spun Yarn From Old Nantucket"—*Wyer, 1914*

SCHOOLS

Schools—*Vol. 39 and 40 G.B.G. Scrapbooks (micro. Athen.)*
Catalogue of Names of All Scholars Who Were Pupils of Nantucket High School
From Its Organization April 16, 1938 to July 1, 1865—*I. & M., Nantucket,*
1865 (pamphlet)
School Supplement—*I. & M., Feb. 2, 1889*
Development of Schools in Nantucket—*N.H.A. Proc. 1903, p. 11*
The Old-Time School—*N.H.A. Proc. 1919, p. 41*
School Argument—*N.H.A. Proc. 1901, p. 18*
Life of Cyrus Peirce—*N.H.A. Proc. 1909, p. 41*
High School Started 1838—*N.H.A. Proc. 1920*
The Journals of Cyrus Peirce and Mary Swift, 1928 (micro. Athen.)
Dedication of Cyrus Peirce School—*"Argument Settlers", Turner 1966, p. 117*
Nantucket School Study—*Study Staff for Town of Nantucket, July 8, 1957*
The Nantucket Schools—*"History of Nantucket", Starbuck, 1924*
Public Schools Established Here in 1827—*"100 Years on Nantucket",*
I. & M., 1921
Education in Nantucket Schools—*Hist. Nant. Jan., 1960*
Cent Schools—*N.H.A. Proc. 1908, p. 41, and "History of Nantucket", Starbuck,*
1924, p. 606

Coffin School—*Recording by Appleton and Gurley (N.H.A.)*
Coffin School—*N.H.A. Proc. 1901, p. 16*
Coffin School—*Booklet Published by Coffin School Assoc. n.d.*
The Coffin School Record—*Newspaper Published 1884-1885*
The Sea Chest, later The Islander—*Newspaper Published by High School Pupils.*
 Vol. 1, No. 1 was Dec., 1926
Nautical School—*N.H.A. Proc. 1902, p. 20*

SCRAPBOOKS

Scrapbooks—*Gardner, Hist. Nant., Apr. 1957*
Scrapbooks—*Recording by Gardner 1959 (N.H.A.)*
61 Scrapbooks on Nantucket Subjects (numbered through 53) Prepared by
 Grace Brown Gardner as listed below: (micro. Athen.)
 listed below: (micro. Athen.)
 1. Churches I.
   General. Baptist. Christian Science. Congregational. Episcopal.
 2. Churches II.
   Friends. Methodist. Roman Catholic. Unitarian. 'Sconset Chapel.
   Others.
 3. General I.
   Farming. Animals. Shearing. Birds. Plants.
 4. General II.
   Anecdotes. Entertainments. Humor. Weather. Miscellaneous.
 5. General III.
   Architecture. Hotels etc. Skipper. Nantucket Books.
 6. Historical I.
   General Migrations. Districts.
 7. Historical II.
   Automobiles. Railroads. Town Clock. Pumps. Industries. Streets.
   Houses.
 8. Land Booms.
 9. Marine I.
   Lightships. Lighthouses. Coast Guard.
 10. Marine II.
   Island Steamers.
 11. Marine III.
   Wrecks.
 12. Marine IV.
   Freeze-Ups. Coasters. Fisheries.
 13. Marine V.
   Quarterboards. Sailors. Blackfish. Wharves. Bathing Beach.
   Training Ship. Cocoanut Oil. Miscellaneous.
 14. Nantucket Cottage Hospital I.
   To 1930.
 15. Nantucket Cottage Hospital II.
   1930.
 16. Nantucket Historical Association I.
   General. Gams.
 17. Nantucket Historical Association II.
   Activities.
 18. Nantucket Historical Association III.
   Exhibits. Fair St. Old Mill. Oldest House.
 19. Nantucket Historical Association IV.
   Exhibits. Whaling Museum. Old Jail. 1800 House. Old North Cemetery
   (see Organizations). 'Sconset Pump. (see also Siasconset).
 20. Nantucket Indians.
 21. Old People's Home.
 22. Organizations I.
   Atheneum.
 23. Organizations II.

53. Whaling IV.
    Whalemen.
Daughters of the American Revolution
Fifty Famous Nantucketers
Genealogical
Ocean House I
Ocean House II
Who's Who in Nantucket
Civil Veterans' Stories
Bird Tracks
    (micro. Athen.)

SCRIMSHAW

"Susan's Teeth"—*Crosby, 1955 (Athen.)*
Scrimshaw—*Crosby, I. & M. Oct. 10, 1958*
Whale Ear Bone—*Crosby, Hist. Nant., Jan. 1957*
Folk Art of the American Whaleman—*Winslow, Hist. Nant. July, 1954 and
    N.H.A. pamphlet 1954*
"Scrimshaw at Mystic"—*Stackpole, 1958*
Extensive Collection Scrimshaw (Whaling Museum)
Other Collections (Athen.—Fair St. Museum—Private Homes in Nantucket)
9 Tiny Ivory Mortar and Pestle Sets Carved by Capt. Charles Murphey on Board
    Whaleship Sophia in 1832 (Whaling Museum) See N.H.A. Proc. 1948, p. 19

SEAL, TOWN OF NANTUCKET

Town Seal—*Coffin, Hist. Nant., Jan. 1959*
Painting of Town Seal by Alexander H. Seaverns (east wall Office of Town
    Clerk, Nantucket)

SEALS

Nantucket Horseheads—*Contribution No. 49, The Hatheway School of
    Conservation Education, Mass. Audubon Society, Lincoln, Mass. N.D.*
American Sealers—*"The Voyage of the Huron and the Huntress", Stackpole,
    1955*
Sealing Voyage, Logbook of Brig Homer 1858-59 (micro. Whaling Museum)

SELDEN, CHARLES A.

Biography by Dr. William E. Gardner (Athen.)

SELECTMEN

Have Served as Selectmen Since 1871—*"100 Years on Nantucket", I. & M. 1921*

SETTLERS, EARLY

House Lots of Settlers—*N.H.A. Bull., Vol. 2, Bull. 2*
Original Lay-Outs on Harbor—*N.H.A. Bull. Vol. 2, Bull. 4*
White Settlers and the Settlement—*"Nantucket: a History", Douglas-Lithgow,
    1914*
"Early Settlers of Nantucket"—*Hinchman, 1896 (Athen.)*
Salisbury Settlers—*"Nantucket Odyssey", Guba, 1951*
House Lot Sections 1661—*1663 and 1665-1680, roughly drawn (Drawer of
    Case 4 (G) Fair St. Museum)*

SHEEP AND SHEARING

See Industries
Sheep and Shearing—*"100 Years on Nantucket", I. & M. 1921*
Copy of Paul Starbuck's Sheep Book, 1742-1743 (Vault, Fair St. Museum)
Sheep Report—*I. & M., Mar. 23, 1834*
Sheep Storm—*I. & M., July 3, 1969 (editorial)*

SHEEP COMMONS

See Land

SHELLFISH

Fish, Shellfish and Lobsters—*Recording by Arthur McCleave and Joe King, 1959 (N.H.A.)*
"The Outer Lands"—*Sterling, 1967*

SHERBURNE

See Settlers, Early

SHIP BUILDING

Ship Building—*"The Island of Nantucket", Godfrey 1882, p. 284*
"A View of Brant Point" showing ship-building. Painting by James Walter Folger (Fair St. Museum)

SHIP MODELS

Model of Whaleship Essex—*made by Capt. H. Percy Ashley (Whaling Museum)*
Model of Whale-boat—*made by Capt. H. Percy Ashley (Whaling Museum)*
Meader Whale Ship Model—*made by William Meader of Nantucket in 1765 when 14 years of age. Believed by the late Charles M. Gay, Marine Curator of Franklin Institute, Phila. to be much the earliest model now in existence of an American whaleship. The old rigging was replaced in 1941 by Charles Sayle and Nikita Carpenko, master ship model builders of Nantucket. (Whaling Museum)*
Model of Clipper "Red Jacket" (Whaling Museum)
Model of Whale Ship "Falcon" (Whaling Museum)
Model of Whaling Bark "Morning Star" of New Bedford (Captains' Room, Whaling Museum)
Other models of various types and periods of both whaling and Merchant ships (Whaling Museum)
Model "Benjamin Packard" (Main Floor Athen., on loan from Robert Leadbetter)
Model "Charles W. Morgan" (Main Floor Athen., on loan from Robert Leadbetter)
Model "Bounty" (Main Floor Athen., on loan from Robert Leadbetter)
Half Hull Ship Model (Main Floor Athen. on Permanent Loan from Robert Waggaman)
Model of "Lagoda of New Bedford" (Children's Room Athen. on Permanent Loan from Robert Waggaman)
Model of Ship Essex (Starr Lawrence Kynett Memorial Room, Athen.)
Model of a Sloop of War, Made by a Prisoner of War (Fair St. Museum)
Half Hull Model Ship Navigator of Nantucket, 1841 (Tap Room Jared Coffin House, Nantucket)
Collections of Ship Models (Charles Sayle, model maker; and private ownership in Nantucket)

SHIPPING LISTS

Shipping Lists 1843 through 1893 in 40 bound volumes (Whaling Museum)
Various Shipping Lists—*(Macy Bldg., Hist. Trust, Nantucket)*

SHIP WRECKS

See Wrecks

SIASCONSET

Plat of Village of Siasconset Accepted at a Meeting of Proprietors 23rd 5 mo. 1835—*Proprietors' Book of Plans #1, p. 76 (Registry Deeds, Nantucket)*
Siasconset Pump—*Shown on Plat above. Early Photograph of Pump in "Early Nantucket and Its Whale Houses", Forman, 1966.*
Siasconset—*Vol. 41 and 42 G.B.G. Scrapbooks (micro. Athen.)*
"The Heart of 'Sconset"—*Hanaford, 1890*
"Evolution of 'Sconset"—*Hussey, 1912*
" 'Sconset in a Nutshell"—*Underhill, n.d.*
"A Picture Booke of Ye Patchwork Village, 'Sconsett By Ye Sea"—*Underhill, E. T. & Co., New York, 1885*

"The Credible Chronicles of the Patchwork Village"—*E. T. & Co., Underhill, 1886*

"Laws of Siasconset, a Ballade"—*1797 and 1822*

Map of Village of Siasconset 1888—*Harry Platt (Fair St. Museum and Lib. Cong. Map Division)*

"'Sconset Cottage Life"—*Northrup, 1901*

Siasconset's Gala Week—*I. & M. Supplement, 1903*

Special 'Sconset Edition of I. & M., May 17, 1947

The 'Sconset Clubhouse—*N.H.A. Proc. 1920, p. 33*

Siasconset—*"The Island of Nantucket", Godfrey, 1882, p. 285*

Siasconset—*"The Far-Away Island", Stevens, 1936*

Moby Dick News, Siasconset, June 27, 1947

Vanished 'Sconset Houses on Nantucket—*Forman, Hist. Nant. Jan., 1959*

"The Old Houses on 'Sconset Bank"—*Forman, 1961*

"'Sconset Actor Colony"—*Recording by Wilson, 1959 (N.H.A.)*

"'Sconset Heyday"—*Barnes, 1969*

"50 Views of Siasconset"—*McIntosh, 1904*

"Views of Nantucket Actors' Colony"—*Murphy, 1904*

"Early Nantucket and Its Whale Houses"—*Forman, 1966*

SIGNS, STREET

Old Street Signs—*"Books and Baskets, Signs and Silver of Old-Time Nantucket", Crosby, 1940*

SILVER AND SILVERSMITHS

The Art of Nantucket Silversmiths—*The Gam 1959—Hist. Nant. Apr. 1959*

Early Nantucket Silversmiths—*Morgan, N.H.A. Proc. 1926*

"Books and Baskets, Signs and Silver of Old-Time Nantucket"—*Crosby, 1940*

"The Spoon Primer"—*Crosby, 1941*

Collections of Nantucket-made Silver (Fair St. Museum; Starr Lawrence Kynett Memorial Room, Athen.; Hadwen House-Satler Memorial; and in many homes in Nantucket)

300 Minute Silver Spoons in a Cherry-Stone, made in Nantucket by Moses Joy Jr. (Fair St. Museum)

SKATING RINK

Skating Rink—*"100 Years on Nantucket", I. & M. 1921*

SLAVERY

Arthur Cooper, a Rescued Slave—*Stackpole, N.H.A. Proc. 1941. Also 1900, p. 5, and 1938, p. 24*

SLIDES

See Pictures

SNAKES

Snakes on Nantucket—*"Nantucket, the Far-Away Island", Stevens, 1936, p. 265*

SOCIETIES

See Organizations

SOCIETY FOR THE PRESERVATION OF NEW ENGLAND ANTIQUITIES

141 Cambridge Avenue, Boston, Mass.

Located in the Library of the Society is a large collection of Nantucket Miscellanea, as noted by Prof. Eugene George in report to Nantucket Historical Trust Aug. 30, 1967. An important part of this material has been reproduced for the Trust and given by them to the N.H.A., as follows:

Blueprints for Restoration Jethro Coffin House, Moors End and House on Gull Island, Nantucket. Also 48 photographs of Nantucket Houses, mostly during restoration. (Fair St. Museum)

SOUNDS

Sounds of Nantucket Island—*Recorded and Narrated by Henry Coffin Carlisle, 1959. Record Sold for Benefit Hospital Thrift Shop, Nantucket (Athen.)*

SPINNING WHEELS

Flax Wheel, Wool Wheel, Swifts and Accessories (1800 House)

STARBUCK

"Three Bricks and Three Brothers"—*Gardner, 1945*

Mary Starbuck Account Book With the Indians, 1662 (Rare Items Vault Fair St. Museum)

Mary Coffin Starbuck—*"Women of the Century"*, Hanaford, 1876; *N.H.A. Proc. 1912; "Nantucket, the Far-Away Island", Stevens, 1936*

Starbuck, William B., Journal 1870-73 (micro. Athen.)

The First Whaling Merchant of Nantucket, Nathaniel Starbuck—*N.H.A. Proc. 1915*

Starbuck, Alexander—*N.H.A. Proc. 1922*

Deed of Edward Starbuck (Manuscript Coll. Fair St. Museum)

Account Books of Thomas Starbuck (Fair St. Museum)

STEAMERS

Steamers—*Vol. 10, G.B.G. Scrapbooks (micro. Athen.)*

Nantucket Steamboat Co.—*N.H.A. Proc. 1899, p. 12*

"The Story of the Island Steamers"—*Turner, 1910*

The Island Steamers—*"Nantucket: a History", Douglas-Lithgow, 1914*

Island Steamboats—*"100 Years on Nantucket", I. &. M. 1921*

"Island Home" Steamer, 1st Arrival of—*N.H.A. Proc. 1937, p. 14*

Gam re Steamboats—*Hist. Nant. Apr. 1957*

The New Steamer "Nantucket" and The Story of the Island Steamers—*2 full pages with photos, I. & M. May 4, 1957*

The Island Steamboat Line—*Hist. Nant., Jan. 1960*

Mr. Lincoln's Flagship: the "River Queen"—*Stackpole, Yankee Magazine, Feb. 1969*

Logbook of Steamer B. G. Wood, chartered by Capt. L. C. Overman, 1878 (micro. Athen.)

Pictures of Steamers at Fair Street Museum include:

"Telegraph", painting by James Walter Folger, from original painting believed to have been by Hinckley.

"Island Home", painting by Wendell Macy

"Island Home Forcing the Ice Bulkhead"—*photograph*

Steam Tug "A. H. Glover" Lost Off Provincetown—*drawing by E. F. Whitman*

Steamer Susquehanna (all above at Fair St. Museum)

2 Photographs of Steamer "New Bedford"—*Hist. Nant., Apr. 1969*

STORMS

Storms and Hurricanes—*Vol. 46, G.B.G. Scrapbooks (micro. Athen.)*

Hurricane 1938—*"Argument Settlers", Turner 1966, p. 134*

Hurricane "Carol"—*"Argument Settlers", Turner, 1966, p. 158*

"Great Storms and Shipwrecks of the New England Coast", Snow, 1943

Storm of Wed., Feb. 27, 1952—*I. & M. Supplement, Mar. 15, 1952*

STREETS

A List of the Names of the Streets, Lanes, Alleys, Courts and Wharves in the Town of Nantucket. Taken by Isaac Coffin, Principal Assessor in 1799 (Book 24, Folio 133, Registry Deeds, Nantucket)

Nantucket Streets—*Worth, N.H.A. Bull. Vol. 2, Bull. 5 (Compiled in 1906 from 1799 list above)*

"A Plat of the Roads in the Town Pasture Laid Out by the Agents of the Proprietors", Nantucket, 10 mo. 27th, 1821—*Proprietors' Book of Plans #1, p. 72 (Registry Deeds, Nant.)*

Paving Streets and Curbstones—*Nantucket Selectmen's Records Sept. 16, 1822*

and Feb. 20, 1840 (Town Clerk's Office, Nantucket)
Map Showing Changes Made in Streets After Fire of 1846 (Map Drawer,
    Registry Deeds, Nantucket)
Main Street—*N.H.A. Proc. 1917, p. 36*
Broad and Gay Streets—*N.H.A. Proc. 1923*
Nantucket Sreets and Lanes, with Old Names—*N.H.A. Proc. 1929, p. 49*
Street Lighting in Nantucket—*Hist. Nant., Oct. 1967*
"Ninety Five Per Cent Perfect"—*Crosby, 1937*
"Rambling Through the Streets and Lanes of Nantucket"—*Stackpole, 1947 and
    1951*
Streets—*Vol. 7 G.B.G. Scrapbooks (micro. Athen.)*

SURFSIDE

Map of Surfside by Rufus Cook—*The Nantucket Surfside Co. Plans for Develop-
    ment, 1873 (Rare Book Room, Boston Public Library)*

SURVEY

Report and Plan of Survey of Island of Nantucket—*U.S. Sec. of War, Jan. 18,
    1828*
Changes in the Ocean Shore-Lines of Nantucket Island—*U.S. Coast and Geodetic
    Survey, Washington, 1893*

SWAIN

Swain Family Reunion—*Hist. Nant. Oct. 1959*
William Swain, Artist—*see Portraits*

T

TAXATION

"A Looking-Glass for the Times"—*Peter Folger, 1878 (Reprint in "Nantucket in
    Print", Crosby, 1946*
See Boston Tea Party

TEA-PARTY

For Boston Tea Party, see Boston
Nantucket's First Tea—*F. C. Sanford (manuscript) (Athen.)*
"An Idyl from Nantucket"—*Collyer, 1885*
"The First Nantucket Tea-Party—*Tittle, 1907*
"An Island Idyll"—*Coleman, New England Magazine, 1907*
Nantucket's First Cup of Tea—*The Atlantic Monthly, n.d.*
"Nantucket's First Tea"—*Turner, I. & M. Press, 1926, 1937, 1938*
"A Nantucket Ghost Walks Again—Over the Teacups"—*Freehafer, 1940*
The "First" Nantucket Tea Party—*A.M.C., Hist. Nant., Oct. 1964*

TELEPHONE, TELEGRAPH AND WIRELESS

Opening of the Nantucket Telephone Cable—*Spalding, 1916 (Crosby Coll.)*
Nantucket's Early Telegraph Service—*Turner, N.H.A. Proc. 1917, p. 39*
First Message from Island—*N.H.A. Proc. 1917, p. 27*
First Trans-Atlantic Station at 'Sconset—*N.H.A. Proc. 1917, p. 47*
Connecting Nantucket With the Mainland—*"100 Years on Nantucket" I. & M.
    1921*
The Great Hall (with photo of first telephone conversation with America)—
    Hist. Nant. Apr., 1957

TELESCOPE, HON. WALTER FOLGER JR.'S

"The Clock That Talks"—*Gardner, 1954*
Restoration of Telescope—*Hist. Nant. Jan. 1955*

THEATRE
Theatre Workshop, Nantucket—*(Files of Workshop, and Newspaper Publicity)*

THOREAU
Thoreau at Nantucket—*Hist. Nant., Apr. 1957, p. 14*

THREE HUNDRED YEARS
Nantucket's 300 Years—*I. & M. Supplement, 1959*

TITHING MEN
Tithing Men—*N.H.A. Proc. 1906*

TITLE TO NANTUCKET ISLAND
King of England to Lord Sterling—*"History Nantucket", Starbuck, 1924, p. 13, and "Albany Papers", Hough, 1856*
Sale of Island to Thomas Mayhew—*"Albany Papers", Hough, 1856*
Sale of Island to Ten Proprietors—*"History of Nantucket", Starbuck, 1924, p. 18*

TOM NEVERS HEAD
Tom Nevers—*"The Island of Nantucket", Godfrey, 1882, p. 315*

TOM THUMB'S VISIT TO NANTUCKET
General Tom Thumb's Three Year Tour Around the World—*New York, 1872 (Athen.)*

TOPAZ, SHIP
Log-Book of Ship Topaz (micro. Whaling Museum)
Log of Ship Topaz at Whaling Museum—*Nelson, "The Nantucket Whaling Museum", N.H.A. Publication, 1955, p. 27*
Finding of Mutineers of Ship Bounty—*N.H.A. Proc. 1918*
Topaz—*"The Story of Yankee Whaling", Shapiro & Stackpole, 1959*

TOURISM
See Resort

TOWN CLERK
Records in Office of Town Clerk:
Vital Statistics, Birth, Deaths and Marriages
Town Reports
Minutes of Town Meetings
Records of Registrars of Voters
Election Returns
Painting of Town Seal

TOWN HOUSE

The Town House and Town Meeting—*"Nantucket: a History", Douglas-Lithgow, 1914*

Town House (first Mentioned in Records)—*"History of Nantucket", Starbuck, 1924*

TOWN RECORDS

See Each Town Department: Assessors; Town Clerk; Registry of Deeds etc.

TRANSPORTATION

See Airport

See Automobiles

See Railroad

See Steamers

Transportation—*Subject of Winter Gam—Hist. Nant., Apr. 1957*

Horse Conveyances—*Hist. Nant., Apr. 1957, p. 36, and "100 Years on Nantucket", I. & M. 1921*

TRAVELS

"Travels Through the Northern Part of the United States"—*Edward A. Kemble, 1809, 3 vol. (Lib. Cong.)*

See Crévecoeur; Emerson and Quincy

TREES ON NANTUCKET

"Geology of Nantucket"—*Shaler, U.S. Dept. Interior, Bull. #43, 1889*

Evidence as to the Former Existence of Large Trees on Nantucket Island—*Burt G. Wilder in Proceedings of the American Association for the Advancement of Science, Aug., 1894*

Trees—*"The Island of Nantucket", Godfrey, 1882, p. 321*

Was Nantucket Ever Forested?—*N.H.A. Proc. 1935, p. 19*

"New Trees or No Trees"—*Reppa, Nantucket Civic League, I. & M. Press, 1945*

"Trees and Shrubs of Nantucket"—*Rice, 1946 and 1967*

Napoleon Willows—*N.H.A. Proc. 1920; Hist. Nant. Apr. 1961; and I. & M. Aug. 15, 1925*

Also see Flora and Fauna

TUCKERNUCK

Tuckernuck—*Vol. 31, G.B.G. Scrapbooks (micro. Athen.)*

Tuckernuck "as divided" 8th mo. 1822—*Proprietors Book of Plans #1, p. 79 (Registry Deeds, Nantucket)*

"Tuckernuck"—*Emma V. Hallett, Plimpton Print, Hartford, 1882 (N.H.A.)*

Tuckernuck—*Worth, N.H.A. Bull., Vol. 2, Bull. 1*

Tuckernuck "Yoho"—*N.H.A. Proc. 1921, p. 51*

The Four Winds—*I. & M. Oct. 6, 1923*

"The Story of Tuckernuck"—*Stark, 1959*

Early Tuckernuck—*Recording by Gurley, 1959 (N.H.A.)*

Tuckernuck—*Recording by Ramsdell, 1959 (N.H.A.)*

Tookanook Island—*Crude Drawing by Eliza Gardner, c. 1829 (Fair St. Museum)*

U

UTILITIES

Gas and Lighting—*I. & M. Jan. 23, and Nov. 24, 1854*

Gas and Electric Co.—*"Argument Settlers", Turner, 1966, p. 116-117*

Sewers—*Records on File in Nantucket Public Works Dept. Office*

Report of Special Committee on Sewerage—*Selectmen's Records Apr. 22, 1910 and Oct. 30, 1926*

Organizations—*Vol. 26, G.B.G. Scrapbooks, (micro. Athen.)*

See Water Co.

V

VANES

The Vanes of Nantucket—*Starbuck, St. Nicholas Magazine, July, 1898*
Old Weather Vane Collection (Fair St. Museum)

VITAL RECORDS

"Vital Records of Nantucket to the Year 1850"—*5 volumes of Births, Deaths and Marriages—Published by New England Historical Genealogical Society, Boston, 1925-1928 (Athen.)*
Vital Statistics—*N.H.A. Proc. 1917, p. 25*
Vital Records (Office of Town Clerk, Nantucket)
Vital Statistics (Library, Fair St. Museum)

VISITORS, FAMOUS

Famous Visitors—*Vol. 46, G.B.G. Scrapbooks (micro. Athen.)*

W

WAGONS

Old Type Wagons & Sleighs—*(Basement, Fair St. Museum)*

WALES

See Milford Haven

WALKS

Roof Walks—*N.H.A. Proc. 1925, p. 10*
"Ninety Five Per Cent Perfect", Crosby, 1937
"A Mirror of Nantucket", Fowlkes, 1959

WARS

Wars—*Vol. 47-48-49 G.B.G. Scrapbooks (micro. Athen.)*
Nantucket in the Revolution—*Starbuck, History & Genealogical Register, 1874-1875*
Nantucket Men Who Served in the Revolution—*"History of Nantucket", Starbuck, 1924, p. 255*
Revolutionary War Service Roll—*Hist. Nant., July, 1963*
Memorial Unveiled to Nantucket Men Who Served Under John Paul Jones in Revolution—and to Lieut. Alexander B. Pinkham—*N.H.A. Proc. 1908, p. 7*
Nantucket's Part in the Revolution—*Gardner, New England Magazine, Jan. 1905*
Naval Records of American Revolution—*U.S. Library Congress, 1906 (Athen.)*
Nantucket's Great Crisis—*N.H.A. Proc. 1929, p. 33*
Nantucket in the Revolution, Spanish War, Civil War, War of 1812 and the

Great World War—*"100 Years on Nantucket", I. & M. 1921*

War of 1812—*"The Island of Nantucket", Godfrey, 1882, p. 202*

Civil War Centennial and Memoranda—*Hist. Nant. Apr. and Oct., 1961*

Nantucket Civil War Veterans' Stories—*Vol. 61, G.B.G. Scrapbooks (micro. Athen.)*

Peace Extra—*I. & M. Supplement, Nov. 11, 1918*

Revolutionary War Pension File of Robert Calder—*Guba, Hist. Nant., Apr. 1969*

2 Swords Used by Lieut. Leander Alley of Nantucket, hero at Fredericksburg in War Between the States (Fair St. Museum) See N.H.A. Proc. 1948, p. 17

WATER

The Fresh Water Supply at Nantucket—*Nantucket Foundation Inc. Bulletin #2, 1940 (Foundation Files)*

Wannacomet Water Co., Founded—*N.H.A. Proc. 1937, p. 30*

Water Works—*The Island of Nantucket", Godfrey, 1882*

History of Wannacomet Water Co.—*Paper by Edgar F. Orpin (Wannacomet Water Co. Files)*

Service Water Network—*1890 Map of Town of Nantucket, by Wm. F. Codd (Wannacomet Water Co. Files)*

WATERFRONT

See Wharves

WAUWINET

Pocomo Through Wauwinet—*Vol. 32 G.B.G. Scrapbooks (micro. Athen.)*

"The Legend of Wauwinet"—*Baxter, I. & M. Press, 1876 (Athen.)*

Wauwinet—*"Nantucket Odyssey", Guba, 1951*

WEATHER

Weather—*Vol. 4, G.B.G. Scrapbooks (micro. Athen.)*

Weather Bureau—*"100 Years on Nantucket", I. & M. 1921*

Nantucket's Underground Moon—*Crosby, N.H.A. Proc. 1941*

"Nantucket Weather"—*Crosby, 1947*

Weather Bureau—*Recording by Grimes, 1959 (N.H.A.)*

Frost Every Month of Year 1816—*"Argument Settlers", Turner 1966, p. 25*

Weather Vanes—*see Vanes*

WEBSTER

Daniel Webster at Nantucket—*N.H.A. Proc. 1933, p. 23*

WESCO

Wesco Acre Lots (Sherburne Bluffs) 1678-1682—*Proprietors' Book of Plans #1, p. 63 (Registry Deeds, Nantucket)*

WHALE HOUSES

"Early Nantucket and Its Whale Houses"—*Forman, 1966*

WHALE CRAFT SHOP

See Whaling Museum

WHALESHIPS

"Life in a Whaleship"—*Delano, 1846*

Commercial News Room's Record of Arrivals and Departures, 1854 (Whaling Museum)

"Whalers and Whaling"—*Chatterton, 1926, p. 139*

List of Equipment in Whale-Boat—*"The Story of Yankee Whaling", Shapiro & Stackpole, 1959*

Whaleship Building—*Jones, Hist. Nant., Jan. 1966*

Layout of a Whaleship's Top Deck and Fitting for Sea—*Hist. Nant., July, 1967*

Whaleship Flags—*see Flags*

Whaleship Logbooks—*see Logbooks*

WHALING

Whaling—*Vol. 50-54 G.B.G. Scrapbooks (micro. Athen.)*
The Whale Fishery—*"American Museum", Phila., Pa. 1789*
"Journal of a Cruise of the U. S. Schooner Dolphin in Pursuit of the Mutineers of the Whale Ship Globe"—*Paulding, 1831*
The American Whale Fishery—*Lanman, Hunt's Merchants Magazine, Nov., 1840*
Whales and Whale Fishing—*Eliza Cook's Journal, 1854*
Whaling Directory of U. S.—*Taber Bros. 1869*
Report Upon the Invertebrate Animals of Vineyard Sound and Adjacent Waters—*Verrill and Smith, 1874 (Athen.)*
Beginnings of the Whale Fishery—*"Men and Manners in America 100 Years Ago", Scudder, 1876*
"Catalogue of Nantucket Whalers"—*Hussey & Robinson, 1876*
"Thrilling Whaling Voyage Journal on Board Ship Dauphin"—*Murphey, 1877*
"History of American Whale Fishery"—*Starbuck, 1878 (micro. Athen.)*
The Perils and Romance of Whaling—*Gustave Kobbe, Century Magazine, 1890*
Bedford, First to Show Stars and Stripes in English Waters—*N.H.A. Proc. 1897*
"The Story of New England Whalers"—*Spears, 1908*
"Whale Fishery of New England"—*Forbes, State Street Trust Co., 1915*
Rise and Fall of Nantucket as a Whaling Port—*"100 Years on Nantucket", I. & M. 1921*
"Whale Ships and Whaling"—*Dow, 1925*
"Whalers and Whaling"—*Chatterton, 1926*
"Whale Ships and Whaling"—*Church, 1938*
"The Yankee Whaler"—*Ashley, 1938*
Old Whaling Days—*Stackpole, N.Y. Times, Mar. 13, 1938 (Ship Oeno and Others)*
Whalemen of Nantucket and Their South Sea Island Discoveries—*N.H.A. Proc. 1945*
Yankee Ship Sailing Cards—*Forbes, State Street Trust, 1948, 1949 and 1952*
Material on Whaling—*T. H. Jenkins in British Museum, 1949*
Whaling (with illustrations of different species of whales)—*"Nantucket Odyssey", Guba, 1951*
"The Sea Hunters"—*Stackpole, 1953*
"Yankee Whalers in the South Seas"—*Whipple, 1954*
Ship Spermo of Nantucket—*Hist. Nant., Jan. 1957*
"The Story of Yankee Whaling"—*Shapiro & Stackpole, American Heritage, 1959*
Whaling—*Recording by Will Tripp, 1959 (N.H.A.)*
"Returns of Whaling Vessels Sailing From American Ports,, 1876-1928"—*Reginald B. Hegerty, 1959*
The Allan Forbes Collection Whaling Prints—*Hist. Nant., Apr. 1961*
Whale Money—*Howard, Yankee Magazine, Oct., 1964*
Also see Sanford

WHALING LOGS

See Logbooks

WHALING MASTERS AND WHALEMEN

Whalemen's Shipping Lists from 1843 through 1893—*40 bound books, indexed (Whaling Museum)*
"Catalogue of Nantucket Whalers"—*Hussey & Robinson, 1876*
"Whaling Masters"—*Old Dartmouth Hist. Soc. 1938*
Addendum to "Starbuck" and "Whaling Masters"—*compiled by Reginald B. Hegerty 1964 (micro. Athen.)*
The First Whaling Merchant of Nantucket—*N.H.A. Proc. 1915*
Whalemen's Adventures—*Stackpole, I. & M. Aug. 25, 1953*
"Voyage to the Pacific"—*Comstock, 1838*
"Life of Samuel Comstock, the Terrible Whaleman"—*William Comstock, 1840 (N.H.A.)*

The Nantucket Whalers and Their Insurance—*News Letter Insurance Society of New York, Dec. 1934*

WHALING MUSEUM

Whaling Museum—*Descriptive Folders Published by N.H.A.*
Whaling Museum Building—*History Done for H.A.B.S. 1967 (Athen.)*
"The Nantucket Whaling Museum"—*Macy, 1929 (pamphlet)*
Formal Opening and Dedication—*N.H.A. Proc. 1930*
Archives at Whaling Museum—*N.H.A. Proc. 1943, p. 30*
Whaling Museum Restoration—*Hist. Nant., Jan. 1958*
Whaling Museum—*Recording by Archie Cartwright 1959 (N.H.A.)*
Many Relics of Whaling at Nantucket—*N.Y. Herald Tribune, Sun., July 3, 1960*
Whaling Museum—*Vol. 19, G.B.G. Scrapbooks (micro. Athen.)*

WHARF RAT CLUB

See Organizations

WHITE, TIMOTHY

Timothy White—*N.H.A. Proc. 1895, p. 8; 1900, p. 12*

WHARVES

Wharves—*Vol. 13, G.B.G. Scrapbooks (micro. Athen.)*
Wharves and Wharf Lots 1774—*Proprietors' Book of Plans #1, p. 12-13 (Registry Deeds, Nantucket) Also: South Beach Laid Out 1805—p. 23-24.*
Wharves—*"History of Nantucket", Godfrey, 1882, p. 312*
Wharves—*"100 Years on Nantucket", I. & M. 1921*
Wharves—*N.H.A. Proc. 1931, p. 23-28*
Waterfront—*Stackpole, Hist. Nant., Apr. 1965*
Old North Wharf—*Recording by Walling, 1959 (N.H.A.)*
Old North Wharf—*Drawing in Pencil by G. G. Fish 1852 (Fair St. Museum)*
10 Photographic Views of Nantucket Wharves 1900 (Charles F. Sayle)
Aerial Photograph Nantucket Wharves 1930 (Fire Chief's Office, Nantaucket Fire Dept.)
Early Wharves or Piers—*Shown on DesBarres Map of 1776 (Whaling Museum)*

WILLOWS, NAPOLEON

See Flora and Fauna

WILLS AND ESTATES

Wills and Estates—*Worth, N.H.A. Bull., Vol. 2, Bull. 6 & 7*
Copies of Old Wills—*Fair St. Museum*
Copies of Old Wills—*(Mrs. Lewis S. Edgarton, Nantucket)*

WIND-MILLS

Windmills—*"Letters from an American Farmer", Crévecoeur 1782, p. 125*
Mills Appear on "A Plat of the Roads in the Town Pasture" dated 1821—*Proprietors' Book of Plans #1, p. 72 (Registry Deeds, Nantucket)*
Old Mill of Nantucket—*Harper's Weekly, Aug. 16, 1879*
Round Top Grist Mill—*I. & M. Apr. 6, 1935*
Mills—*I. & M. July 25, 1936*
Mill Replacing Shaft—*Hist. Nant., July 1953*
Old Mill—*I. & M. Apr. 22, 1965*
Fulling Mills—*see Industries*

WINSLOW

See Heart of Dr. Winslow

WIRELESS

See Telephones, etc.

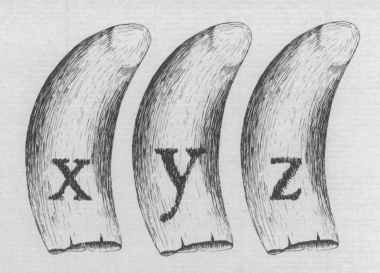

WORTH

Worth Family—*I. & M. July 19, 1873*
Henry B. Worth—*N.H.A. Proc. 1902, p. 6; 1923, p. 35*

WRECKS

"Wrecks Around Nantucket"—*Gardner 1877; 1915, 1930 with added Material by Turner; 1954 with added Material by Sayle.*
Wrecks—*Vol. 11, G.B.G. Scrapbooks (micro. Athen.)*
"Shipwreck of Ship Oswego"—*Paddock, 1818*
"Ship-Wreck of Whale-Ship Essex of Nantucket"—*Owen Chase, 1821*
"Wrecked on the Feejees"—*Compiled from Wm. S. Cary's Logbook, 1922*
"Great Storms and Famous Shipwrecks of New England Coast"—*Snow, 1943*
Wreck of Cabin Cruiser Constance—*I. & M. Sept. 17, 1949*
Andrea Doria in Collision with Stockholm—*Nantucket Town Crier, July 27, 1956*
Wrecks Around Nantucket—*Hist. Nant., Oct. 1960*
Rescue of the Kirkham's Crew—*I. & M. Jan. 26, 1967*

WRITINGS, EARLY

Early Writings About Nantucket—Books to Collect and Books to Read—*"Nantucket in Print", Crosgy, 1946*

WYER FAMILY

The Nantucket Wyers—*James I. Wyer, Privately Printed, New York, 1911 (Athen.)*

Y

YOHO

See Tuckernuck

Z

ZONING

"Ninety Five Per Cent Perfect"—*Crosby, 1937*
"Our Gold Mine"—*Crosby, 1951*
Proposed Zoning By-Law 1967—*I. & M., Jan. 19, 1967*

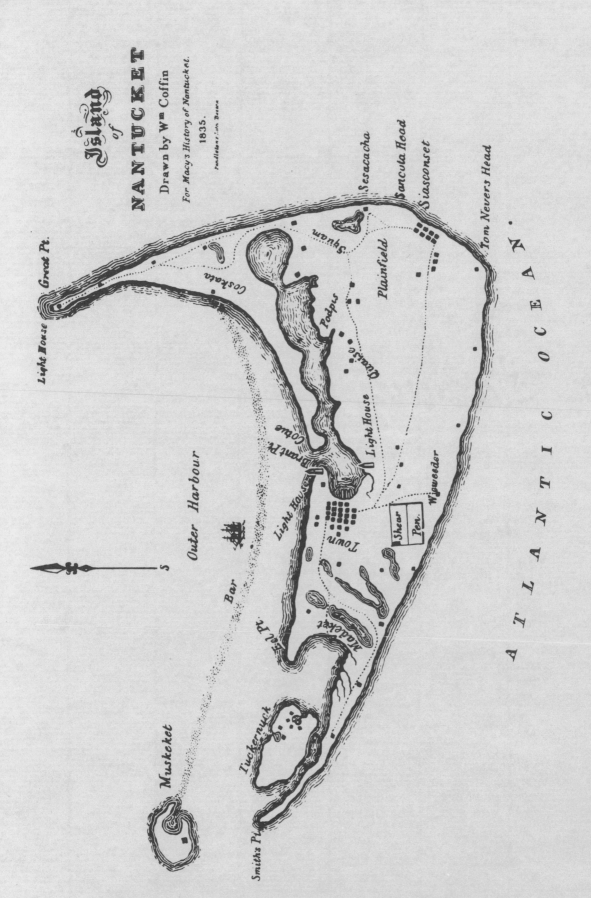

Island of NANTUCKET

Drawn by Wm Coffin

For Macy's History of Nantucket.

1835.

Pendleton's Lith Boston

Light House

Great Pt.

Outer Harbour

Muskeket

Bar

Tuckernuck

Smiths Pt.

Eel Pt.

Coatue

Light House

Madaket

Town

Shear Pen.

Wigwarder

Light House

Coskata

Podpis

Squam

Quaise

Plainfield

Sesacacha

Sancula Head

Siasconset

Tom Nevers Head

ATLANTIC OCEAN.

The text of this book was set in Bookman
type face, with headings and titles in Caslon
Antique. The book was printed in offset on
Kilmory Text, laid finish.

Designed and Produced by

Fred H. Gardner
New York, New York
and
Nantucket, Massachusetts

Printed by

Laros Printing Company
Bethlehem, Pennsylvania

Front end paper: *The Town of Sherburne in the Island of Nantucket.
A view painted by Thomas Birch shortly after 1795 when Sherburne was
changed to Nantucket as the name of the Island's principal town. The old
name was still used by many for some time after.*

Back end paper: *The Town of Nantucket—1839. This engraving by John
W. Barber appeared in his book about the Island, printed in 1839.*

A HARBOR VIEW of t.